Praise for the Bestselling First Edition

"One of the most brilliant, original, and exciting leadership books I've read in a long time. It will be the most useful and concise book on leadership you'll ever read!"
—Warren Bennis, Distinguished Professor of Business, University of Southern California, and author of *Still Surprised: A Memoir of a Life in Leadership*

"With this compact handbook, Mike Useem provides leaders what they all say they want and need but rarely get: a kick-in-the-pants reminder of those parts of the job they have neglected. The boss is now forewarned."
—Steven Pearlstein, former *Washington Post* business columnist and moderator of the "On Leadership" web page

"Leading an enterprise comes down to a set of enduring principles, and *The Leader's Checklist* compellingly captures the most vital. Michael Useem has written *the* essential companion for anybody whose leadership is on the line."
—Ram Charan, advisor to CEOs and boards, and coauthor of the best-sellers *Execution: The Discipline of Getting Things Done* and *The Leadership Pipeline*

"*The Leader's Checklist* reads like an adventure yarn, but packs a goldmine of scholarship and tested observations, that surrounds a list of fifteen principles that guide and teach managers to make on-target, effective business decisions, under real pressure."
—Blogcritics

T0273039

"*The Leader's Checklist* can refresh a leader's sense of purpose as well as invigorate his or her calling to lead others."

—John Baldoni, SmartBlog on Leadership

"*The Leader's Checklist* gets to the point quickly. It may well set the bar for quality writing and amount of content for other business-related digital books in the future."

—Patricia Faulhaber, Suite101

10TH ANNIVERSARY EDITION

Michael Useem

THE
Leader's
Checklist

16 MISSION-CRITICAL PRINCIPLES

WHARTON
SCHOOL
PRESS
Philadelphia

© 2021, 2011 by Michael Useem

Published by Wharton School Press
The Wharton School
University of Pennsylvania
3620 Locust Walk
300 Steinberg Hall-Dietrich Hall
Philadelphia, PA 19104
Email: whartonschoolpress@wharton.upenn.edu
Website: wsp.wharton.upenn.edu/

Ebook ISBN: 978-1-61363-117-1
Paperback ISBN: 978-1-61363-118-8
Hardcover ISBN: 978-1-61363-119-5

Contents

Introduction
Why a Leader's Checklist

A business executive briefs company managers on plans for the coming year, referencing product launches, analyst concerns, and pandemic shocks. The presentation proves engaging and stimulating, yet the moment feels strangely incomplete, an opportunity unfulfilled.

Whether in person or online, managers at the briefing learn little more than they already knew about the speaker personally. They sense nothing about how their boss views them collectively or what is expected of them individually. Even worse, they hear much about the tactics of the moment but little about the longer-term goals they are expected to achieve and the strategies for doing so. The executive weaves together some of the essential threads of a leadership fabric—but falls far short of completing the whole cloth.

Sound familiar? It should. My work on leadership development in the United States and abroad confirms that meetings like this take place all the time in a multitude of languages, to the universal consternation of those present. And often the root cause is simply a lack of experience or preparation, because leading effectively is a composite but learnable skill set acquired through practice, seasoning, and discipline.

The simple expedient of building and mastering the equivalent of a pilot's or a surgeon's mission-critical checklist—the leader's checklist—can lessen many of these leadership lapses so often evident in routine gatherings but even when far more is on the line.

That is why I originally wrote *The Leader's Checklist* and now offer this updated 10th anniversary edition. It's hard to believe that a decade has passed since Wharton School Press first published *The Leader's Checklist*. Interest in the concept has remained keen from the outset. For a week following its initial publication, the press offered the ebook for free across all retailers, and readers downloaded more than 30,000 copies. *The Leader's Checklist* went on to become a *Washington Post* "Best Leadership Book of the Year" and has appeared in Chinese, Korean, and Portuguese.

In the 10 years since this book was first published, I have heard from scores of managers who have held their leadership principles up to the reality of their professional lives and the exigencies of the times they inhabit. From venues far and wide—the United Nations and World Economic Forum, China and India, Mastercard and Medtronic, Google and Netflix—managers have reported on the principles they believe need greater emphasis, further refinement, or even addition or deletion, as well as what struck home with special force. The main principles presented here, I am ever more convinced from that feedback, are timeless and placeless, though like all business conditions, the particular circumstances for the principles' application are always changing, requiring continuous fine-tuning.

Every author of a book such as this hopes the volume will prove useful not only in prosperous times when living is easier but also in hard times when leadership is put to special test. Here is one confirming message for the latter from a manager at a large American corporation that had decided as a matter of business strategy to exit a market it had excelled in for a decade:

> My charge has been to help manage the exit. We are now almost a year into the transition with perhaps two-and-a-half years remaining. With this change, over 1,500 employees have been impacted, but not all at once.
>
> The senior leadership team has the constant challenge of directing, engaging, and retaining employees through the time they are needed to do the critical work of continuing to meet

customer needs as well as wind down the business. In a blink of an eye last year, employees found their work changing, their leaders changing, and of course, their own personal circumstance changing. They went from a growing, ongoing concern for the business to a "below the line" expense that must be cut. And as a result, just as quickly, leaders have had to adapt how they lead.

I have been through divestitures and wind downs in past roles and know of some of the pitfalls that can come along. And as the program manager, I was fully prepared for the worst that could occur from people and financial results. But with this exit, the results have been remarkable. With very little time to strategize and little information to go on, plans have been met within a few percentage points, financial measures have been met or exceeded, and most important, employee satisfaction and engagement have significantly increased.

It has been amazing to watch the growth in leaders as they have had to employ many of the 15 core principles you have outlined. At the time, they didn't do it because they knew it was part of a list; they did it because it was simply the right thing to do for employees and to manage the business. Still, I found it easy to nod in agreement while reading your book since I had in front of me every day real examples of highly effective leadership in action in a very difficult situation.

In this new edition, I seek to lay out an expanded and refined set of indispensable, time-tested leadership principles that vary surprisingly little among companies, countries, or epochs. Taken together, they provide a template for action whatever the enterprise, the moment, or the era.

I will also introduce you to a new 16th principle, which should be considered as universal as any: Think and act as if you are the top leader of an enterprise, working through what your organization would expect of you at that moment even if you are not formally or fully in charge. We will see this play out in the ascension of a manufacturing executive who, in the view of her board chair, already thought like a "CEO before she was *the* CEO."

In Parts I and II, I set forward 16 principles that together constitute that leader's checklist and explore them in action in settings as varied as a company decision on Wall Street, a leadership moment during the US Civil War, an audacious rescue carried out under the glare of international attention, the restructuring of a troubled company, and a Super Bowl run for the Philadelphia Eagles football team. I'll show you how to customize and apply the checklist. I'll provide a glimpse of the lessons we can learn from both the boom times and the challenging times, such as the COVID-19 pandemic—the collective global crisis that forced leaders of nearly every company to respond.

In Part III, I explain how you can build these checklists for your own company and how to apply and modify the principles to better fit your own situation. I end with an owner's manual—a set of prompts intended to assist your readiness to apply the principles.

Applying, testing, and evolving your leadership precepts is indeed essential. Learning to lead is one of those personal capacities improved by repeated application and accumulated experience. Trying and revising your leader's checklist will serve as an indispensable learning cycle to ensure that your principles remain current, complete, and customized for your own challenges.

Should you find yourself in a moment where your courage and your company's mettle are being tested by turbulent markets or growing pains, I hope you too will find *The Leader's Checklist* a useful resource. And now on to the 16 principles that are that template for action.

PART I

Building Your Personal Checklist

Constructing a Checklist

I magine yourself in this situation: Less than five months ago, you were summoned from the private sector to join a newly formed national government. Your background is in consumer retail; now you are regulating the nation's mining industry. You are abroad on a state visit, still working up to speed, when word reaches you from your home office that there has been a mining disaster—a cave-in deep below, death toll unknown, with nearly three dozen people missing.

Or envision this: For decades, your financial services firm has sailed along. Not only have revenues soared, but your company has earned a treasured AAA credit rating while creating an extraordinary wealth engine: a little giant of a division that insures against debt defaults, including subprime mortgages. Continuing prosperity seemed assured, but suddenly the market implodes. Subprime mortgages turn noxious, an investment bank fails, and your AAA rating slips to AA, then A-minus. With those downgrades, you are required to post billions of dollars in collateral that you simply do not have. Your boat is heading for a cataract, and you seem helpless at the tiller.

Or this one: The enemy has surrendered after a four-year conflict that has left more than 700,000 dead, and your commander has ordered you to arrange one of the war's crowning moments, the formal surrender of the enemy's most venerated army. The tone, the

texture of the ceremony, the formalities of receiving the adversary—
they are for you to craft.

And still one more: An industrial manufacturer is breaking itself
into three entities and its board chair asks you, the chief financial
officer, to helm one of the spin-offs. Having minded the parent's
financial shop, you are now summoned to take charge of everything
in the new offspring, from plant operations and product marketing
to human resources and governance practices. Worse, it is a troubled enterprise with asbestos liabilities and without a cohesive identity. Are you ready to turn it around and master it all?

These are not, of course, hypothetical situations. Laurence
Golborne, the new mining minister for the Republic of Chile, was
visiting Ecuador when his chief of staff in Santiago sent him a simple
but urgent text. "Mine cave-in Copiapó," she wrote, with "33 victims."
Twenty-eight hours later, at 3:30 a.m., Golborne arrived at the site of
the mining disaster in the remote Atacama Desert of northern Chile.
Soon, hundreds of millions of people around the globe would be witnessing one of the greatest mine rescues of all time.

Like the miners in Chile, American International Group
(AIG)—a financial services giant heading for a cascade—was ultimately rescued through government intervention. When the subprime mortgage market in which AIG was deeply invested began to
implode, its chief executive found he had put in place too few pro-
tective measures. His tone-deaf response to the tumultuous events
leading up to the global financial crisis left the company vulnerable
to one of the greatest corporate collapses in business history. The
company had been deemed "too big to fail," and now it seemed almost
too toxic to save.

How different were the actions taken by Union officer Joshua
Lawrence Chamberlain when General Ulysses S. Grant handed him
the historic duty of coordinating a follow-up ceremony to Confederate
general Robert E. Lee's surrender at Appomattox, Virginia. Instead
of humiliating the Confederate army, as might have been expected
after four years of deadly conflict, Chamberlain ordered a reunify-
ing salute and launched a healing process that helped rejoin a nation.

Then there's Denise Ramos, the former chief financial officer of ITT. She had a head start, in the view of the chair of her governing board, thanks to her acquired ability to think and act as a general manager—taking responsibility for everything even before she had taken formal responsibility for all. In the years ahead, once fully in charge, she revamped and redirected the spin-off to outperform its market, taking the company, in the words of one equity analyst, to a "very healthy" place."[1]

Three of the leaders we have just met were well prepared when summoned to their moment in history, but one was obviously not. To be sure, few of us are likely to have our leadership tested in such trying ways. But all of us can and should prepare for less public setbacks and turning points in our own ways of serving, and it calls us to ask: Why did Joshua Chamberlain, Laurence Golborne, and Denise Ramos rise so effectively to their challenges? Why, by contrast, was the AIG executive unable to fashion a calamity-preventing or life-saving response? And is the skill set that served Chamberlain, Golborne, and Ramos learnable, transferable, and applicable to other leaders who may never be called to scale the same kinds of mountains that these leaders ascended, but who are sure to face daunting terrains of their own?

A central premise for this book is that we each should be able to offer an affirmative response to those questions. Effective leadership for the personal challenges ahead can be mastered, in my view, by all readers who carry any responsibility for the performance of their enterprises or their teams. That is why I advocate, and in these pages lay out, a mission-critical checklist, a set of the most impactful and essential leadership principles that are tried, tested, and true.

The leader's checklist, we shall see, is composed of a limited set of principles applicable to most managers, in most endeavors, in most circumstances. Given the vast variety of leadership roles, one size does not precisely fit all, but the checklist and its broadly defined components can nonetheless help prepare you for guiding your own enterprise or team through both good times and worst-case scenarios, even if (thankfully) you are never forced to face the latter.

Building the Checklist

To build the leader's checklist, I have tapped not only my own research experience but also that of an array of investigators, thinkers, and practitioners. Working with hundreds of managers and executives in Asia, Europe, North America, and South America, interviewing managers in the United States and abroad, and witnessing managers facing a range of critical moments, I have concluded that their thinking and experience point to a core of mission-critical leadership principles that vary surprisingly little among companies or countries.[2]

From my own reading, too, I have become convinced that with leadership, as with so much else, brevity is the soul of wit. But the checklist also cannot be too skeletal or minimalist. Albert Einstein once described the calling of modern physics as an effort to make the physical universe as simple as possible—but not simpler. The leader's checklist is likewise at its best when it is as bare-bones as possible—though not more so.[3]

My own engagement with participants in a wide range of leadership programs has been critical to identifying these principles. I have asked many managers and executives, for instance, how they would lead or have led, and to test those ideas I have frequently placed managers and executives in a leader's shoes at a particularly challenging moment. I elicit their pragmatic, experience-based knowledge of what is essential for effective exercise of their own leadership during that instant.

One such moment centered on the chief executive of IBM, Virginia Rometty, as she acquired the hybrid cloud-computing company Red Hat for $34 billion. "Most companies today are only 20% along their cloud journey," renting computer power to "cut costs," she explained. The "next 80% is about unlocking real business value and driving growth," and that, she said, "requires shifting business applications to hybrid cloud" and "extracting more data and optimizing every part of the business." On the flip side, Red Hat CEO James Whitehurst explained his embrace of IBM's overture for that purpose while at the same not giving up his firm's identity: "Joining forces with IBM will provide us with a greater level of scale, resources and capabilities," he said, yet at the same time it will also preserve "our unique culture."[4]

By the deal's terms, Red Hat would remain a distinct operation within IBM's Hybrid Cloud Team, though Whitehurst was to report directly to the IBM CEO. Red Hat would maintain its North Carolina home office, even though IBM was headquartered nearly 600 miles north. Many of Red Hat's 13,000 employees were no doubt skeptical about the takeover by a distant company with a different culture that had so far found little traction in the cloud, one of the era's premier emergent technologies; at the time Microsoft held 15% of the cloud-computing market, Amazon 34%, and IBM just 7%.[5]

Imagining that Rometty met with an assemblage of Red Hat—now IBM—employees a few days after their acquisition, I ask a manager or executive to play the role of CEO Rometty at the gathering. I ask others to respond as newly concerned or even reluctant employees of IBM. After a round of questions for the IBM chief executive, I query participants on what they would want and expect to hear from the CEO, their new superior, if they were to remain with the merged companies and devote themselves with gusto to building and running the combination during the months ahead.

Chapter 2

Principles for the Checklist

M ore than a dozen leadership principles emerge from this exercise (see box 2.1), and they do so consistently—whether the managers are working in high technology, investment banking, or public service; whether they are functioning in good times or bad; and whether they are managing in China, India, Japan, or the United States.

Other sources affirm the standing of each of these core principles, including studies of the qualities of leadership by academic investigators, appraisals of leadership development programs by independent parties, and what leaders report has served them well. Here is a brief sampling of such sources.

Principles 1 (Articulate a Vision), 2 (Think and Act Strategically), and 3 (Honor the Room)

Two well-informed observers, educator Howard Gardner and researcher Emma Laskin, explored historical sources on twentieth-century luminaries ranging from Nelson Mandela and Mahatma Gandhi to Margaret Thatcher and George C. Marshall, and they concluded that their common leadership threads included an exceptional ability to define a compelling vision for change, devise a strategy for achieving it, and honor those followers who were being asked to achieve it.[6]

Box 2.1. The Leader's Checklist

1. **Articulate a Vision.** Formulate a clear and persuasive vision and communicate it repeatedly to all members of the enterprise.

2. **Think and Act Strategically.** Set forth a pragmatic strategy for achieving that vision both short- and long-term, and ensure that it is widely understood; consider all the players, and anticipate their reactions and resistance before they are manifest.

3. **Honor the Room.** Frequently express your confidence in and support for those who work with and for you.

4. **Take Charge and Lead Change.** Embrace a bias for action, taking responsibility even if it is not fully or formally delegated, particularly if you are especially well positioned to make a difference.

5. **Act Decisively.** Make good and timely decisions, and ensure that they are executed.

6. **Communicate Persuasively.** Communicate in ways that people will not forget; simplicity and clarity of expression help.

7. **Motivate the Workforce.** Appreciate the distinctive intentions that people bring, and then build on those diverse motives to draw the best from each.

8. **Embrace the Front Lines.** Delegate authority except for strategic decisions, and stay close to those most directly engaged with the work of the enterprise.

9. **Build Leadership in Others.** Develop leadership throughout the organization.

10. **Manage Relations.** Foster enduring personal ties with those who look to you, and work to harness the feelings and passions of the workplace.

11. **Identify Personal Implications.** Help everybody appreciate the impact that the vision and strategy are likely to have on their own work and future with the firm.

12. **Convey Your Character.** Through gesture, commentary, and narratives, ensure that others appreciate that you are a person of transparency and integrity.

13. **Dampen Overoptimism and Excessive Pessimism.** Counter the hubris of success, focus attention on latent threats and unresolved problems, and protect against taking unwarranted risks; at the same time, bolster confidence in coming back from downturns and setbacks.

14. **Build a Diverse Top Team.** Leaders need to take final responsibility, but leadership is also a team sport best played with an able and varied roster of those collectively capable of resolving the key challenges.

15. **Place Common Interest First.** In setting strategy, communicating vision, and reaching decisions, common purpose comes first, personal self-interest last.

16. **Think Like a CEO.** Work through what a company CEO—or even a country's president or top leader—would expect of you at that moment, and bring that expectation into your actions.

Principles 4 (Take Charge and Lead Change)
and 5 (Act Decisively)

The US Marine Corps Officer Candidates School places great emphasis on taking charge and acting decisively. To build an ability to make rapid decisions under stress with incomplete information, would-be Marine commanders learn to make do with a "70%" solution, not 100% consensus or certainty; explain unambiguous objectives and leave their subordinates to work out the details; tolerate mistakes if they point to stronger performance next time and are not repeated; and view indecisiveness as a fatal flaw—worse than making a mediocre decision, because a middling decision, swiftly executed, can at least be corrected. In a similar vein, Warren Bennis, an academic observer and a university administrator, concluded that effective leaders were most often defined by a driving determination to reach a goal, an ability to generate trust and communicate optimism, and a bias for action when ambiguity prevails.[7]

Principle 6 (Communicate Persuasively)

Drawing on what leaders themselves report is also a rich lode. There is no shortage of leaders willing to reveal what has worked, or sometimes failed, in their own exercise of power. Inevitably, some of these accounts are exercises in vanity, self-promotion, or personal justification, but the best of such self-reporting furnishes useful insights from the front lines of leadership. Dawn Lepore, the CEO of an online retailer later acquired by Walgreens, offered that while she was "very comfortable with ambiguity," when "you're leading a large organization, people are not as comfortable with ambiguity, and they want you to be clearer about what's happening, where you're taking them. So I had to get better at communicating what I was thinking." Communicating must also be two-way, reported Carol Bartz, an early CEO of internet provider Yahoo, who saw the act of hearing as essential, if not always natural: "I have a bad habit—you get half your question out and I think I know the whole question, so I want to answer it. And so I actually had to be trained to take a breath. I really want to listen. I want to engage, but I have to shut up."[8]

Principles 7 (Motivate the Workforce), 8 (Embrace the Front Lines), and 9 (Build Leadership in Others)

Peter Drucker, who studied managers in action over six decades, deemed effective leaders to be those who delegated much but retained authority over what was most strategic for the organization. But effective leaders also have a habit of personally visiting the front lines, giving rise to the title of one of Drucker's publications on the subject: "Not Enough Generals Were Killed," a slighting reference to World War I army commanders who remained far from the battle lines while ordering soldiers into lethal rounds of trench warfare. To

Noel Tichy, a university professor who also directed General Electric's leadership program, building the workforce is a matter of creating other leaders throughout the organization. American Express, Procter & Gamble, and many other organizations have created and refined such programs to instill leadership across the ranks.[9]

Principles 10 (Manage Relations), 11 (Identify Personal Implications), and 12 (Convey Your Character)

Frances Hesselbein, who led the Girl Scouts for more than a decade, emphasized the value of personal mentoring, flattening the hierarchy, and hearing dissent. For researcher Daniel Goleman, vital qualities are exceptional self-awareness, self-regulation, and personal empathy, a combination that he has termed "emotional intelligence." An academic team that studied middle managers in financial services, food processing, and telecommunications in 62 countries ranging from Albania to Zimbabwe concluded that leaders should avoid autocratic, egocentric, and irritable styles.[10]

Principles 13 (Dampen Overoptimism and Excessive Pessimism), 14 (Build a Diverse Top Team), 15 (Place Common Interest First), and 16 (Think Like a CEO)

I share accounts later in the book that underscore the value of the four final principles.

Chapter 3

Customizing the Checklist

Taken together, the 16 principles establish a foundation for leadership at most organizations at most times. But "most" is not always good enough. Further customization is also required for distinct times and unique contexts. Among the most important divisions are those of company, role, country, moment, stage, and place.

Company

Every organization requires a partially distinctive set of checklist principles. In recent years, many of the largest have established just that. The leader's checklist for General Electric, for instance, according to those highly familiar with the company, includes teaching others how to lead their divisions, making tough—often wrenching—personnel decisions around performance, and continually innovating. A checklist for Google, by contrast, would place greater emphasis on the individual pursuit of creative sparks, keeping teams small, and guiding others in an even-keeled manner. A checklist for a major professional services firm will require a handful of still different capacities for rising managers—seeing the world through the eyes of clients, engaging with clients, and guiding clients toward unconventional thinking.[11]

Role

Distinct managerial positions necessitate their own unique additions to the core leader's checklist. In interviewing more than a hundred company executives and institutional investors—part of a study of how the two work together or are sometimes at odds with one another—I found a special demand for chief executives who can build personal familiarity with their largest investors, articulate a compelling vision for where the company is going, offer a persuasive strategy for getting there, and generate predictable growth in company earnings. In a separate study of company directors, a professional colleague and I learned that many directors place a premium on partnering with (not just monitoring) management, establishing clear lines between decisions retained by the board and those delegated to management, and taking an active role with management in setting company strategy.[12]

A customized checklist for CEOs would thus include building relations with investors, making a persuasive case for how the company will generate shareholder value, and then delivering steady growth in quarterly and annual earnings. The customized checklist for company directors, by contrast, would include an ability to partner with and monitor company executives, guide company strategy, and create a bright line between delegated decisions and retained authority.

Country

Still other leadership add-ons are essential for varied national locations. What is required in China or India is at least partially distinct from what is essential in America or Brazil. This can be seen in the findings of a study of diverse leadership styles among 67 countries. Working to engage rather than just instruct others drew high marks in countries such as the United States. In China, by contrast, leaders place a greater premium on indirect forms of communication through metaphors and parables.[13]

In pursuit of such customized principles for leading business in India, three colleagues and I interviewed senior executives at 100 of the largest 150 publicly traded Indian companies. Better-known Indian firms included Infosys, Reliance, and Tata. Among our interviewees was R. Gopalakrishnan, executive director of Tata Sons, which oversaw Tata Group, India's largest company in market capitalization, with interests in automobiles, communication, consulting, hotels, power, steel, and tea. Drawing upon his experience in presiding over 300,000 employees and revenue equal to 3% of India's GDP, Gopalakrishnan told us that Indian executives like himself had adopted Western leadership principles but also embraced distinctly Indian qualities in running their enterprises.[14]

For the Indian manager, Gopalakrishnan explained, "His intellectual tradition, his 'y-axis,' is Anglo-American," but "his action vector, his 'x-axis,' is in the Indian ethos." Many "foreigners come to India," he said, "they talk to Indian managers, and they find them very articulate, very analytical, very smart, very intelligent. And then they can't for the life of them figure out why the Indian manager can't do something" as "prescribed by the analysis." Indian business leaders, he concluded, "think in English" but also "act Indian."

While the 16 core leadership principles are largely the same in both the United States and India—company executives in both emphasize company strategy and workforce motivation, both on the y-axis—our study revealed that Indian business leaders embraced four additional principles, all on an x-axis, constituting a kind of extra "India Way" for leading business on that subcontinent, summarized in box 3.1.

We conducted a similar study of business leaders in China, interviewing 72 chief executives and directors of large non-state-owned companies. Five distinct leadership principles of a "China Way" emerged from our study of these companies and their leaders, as seen in box 3.2.[15]

Box 3.1. The India Way

- **Holistic engagement with employees.** Indian business leaders see their firms as organic enterprises where sustaining employee morale and building company culture are critical obligations. People are viewed as assets to be developed, not costs to be pared.

- **Improvisation and adaptability.** Improvisation is also at the heart of the India Way. In a complex, often volatile environment with few resources and much red tape, business leaders have learned to rely on their wits to circumvent innumerable hurdles.

- **Creative value propositions.** Given the large and intensely competitive domestic market, Indian business leaders have of necessity learned to create value propositions that satisfy the needs of demanding but limited-means consumers and do so with extreme efficiency.

- **Broad mission and purpose.** Indian business leaders place special emphasis on personal values, a vision of growth, and strategic thinking. They take pride in not only enterprise success but also family prosperity, regional advancement, and national renaissance.

Box 3.2. The China Way

- **An abiding willingness to embrace uncertainty.**
- **An urgency to capitalize on business opportunities.**
- **Confidence and optimism, with a focus on action.**
- **Patient, persistent, and passionate about company purpose and mission.**
- **Learning business leadership from their own experience and with few historical models.**

Moment

The need for customization of the leader's checklist applies to specific moments as well. What is essential in changing times is at least partially different from what is required in static times. What is needed in hard times varies from the requisite skills for good times.

For leading organizational change, for example, academic John Kotter and consultant Dan Cohen offer an eight-step template—checklist principles that those leading the change would be wise to embrace. These include creation of a compelling rationale for change and taking small steps that pave the way for greater transformation. Each of those steps also requires graphic portrayal, such as hearing directly from distressed customers, for building a "burning platform" for change.[16]

For leading companies during a sharp downdraft, by contrast, consider the customized checklist that emerged from a study of large US firms during the global financial crisis. Along with two colleagues, I interviewed 14 chief executives of major publicly traded American companies at the height of the global financial crisis in 2009. We asked the CEOs what they deemed critical to the leadership of their firms during a period of nearly unprecedented cutbacks, furloughs, and layoffs brought on by the failures of Lehman Brothers, AIG, Merrill Lynch, and other financial firms.

Those interviewed included the chief executives of DuPont, Northrop Grumman, Procter & Gamble, 3M, Travelers, and Tyco. While each emphasized actions unique to his or her own firm, most also stressed eight add-on principles. One, for instance, was to devote extra time and attention to the firm's clientele. As A. G. Lafley, then–chief executive of Procter & Gamble, put it, "A lesson I would give others on how to manage through tough times is to stay close to your customers." Another was to swiftly recognize the hard reality and get on with corrective actions, as Tyco CEO Ed Breen described: "You have to get as much data as quickly as possible. But you will never get it all—so you need to make decisions quickly." Other principles for leading in stressful times, as articulated by this set of chief executives, included reaffirming the mission but confronting reality, concentrating on what you can control, and reinforcing faith in coming back and recovering.[17]

Still other customized checklists are required for leading other kinds of institutions, ranging from universities and nonprofit organizations to religious movements, school systems, sports teams, community services, microfinance institutions such as Women's World Banking, and macroagencies such as the United Nations. Consider Ayla Göksel, the chief executive of the Mother Child Education Foundation, which operates in Turkey and the Middle East on women's empowerment and rural development. She was an experienced social service leader who had reached more than a million beneficiaries during the previous quarter century, and for that, she reported, her leadership template included program diversification and distance learning to reach the underserved, empower families, and advocate policies.[18]

Stage

Although the checklist principles have emerged from research and observations of managers in large organizations, the experience of small-firm managers also points to the importance of developing a specialized leader's checklist for starting and leading fast-growing enterprises.

When Margaret Whitman arrived to build eBay in California, the company employed just 35 people. To her surprise, Whitman found her staff maintained no appointment calendars or virtually any daily structure; none were required for the informal ways in which founder Pierre Omidyar had led the fledgling enterprise. By the time Whitman departed a decade later, however, eBay's payroll had soared to 15,000 employees. In terms of foundational principles, the leadership challenges Whitman faced were unchanged. Strategic thinking remained essential, but now she had added calendars and routines to her package as well.

An equally stark example of radically altered terrain: When Liu Chuanzhi started Lenovo in China in 1984—in a guardhouse at the Chinese Academy of Sciences—he had just two employees, including himself. A quarter century later, he presided over one the world's largest personal computer companies. In its earliest days, the company required no formalities of any kind, but as with eBay, successful growth brought an additional set of principles while simultaneously requiring the continued application of the company's enduring precepts. The latter meant a weekly review of the decisions of the past five days—a process that Liu continued over the decades. By repeatedly looking back to better see forward, the CEO built and refined his leader's checklist—one that later helped his company acquire the IBM personal computer division and emerge onto the world stage. At the same time, newer leadership principles now required Liu's oversight of vast supply chains and multinational branding.

Place

While core and customized principles constitute a kind of "true north" for every manager, each leader's checklist is usefully adapted as well for one's personal place. No two leadership positions are exactly the same, nor do any two circumstances require the identical exercise of leadership. By way of illustration, here are three checklists that have been customized for personal place.

Patrolling

A commanding officer created a set of checklists for his US infantry units operating in Afghanistan. Termed "tactical standard operating procedures," they referenced actions required of officers operating in the field at a variety of points, ranging from reconnaissance and bivouacking to escalating force and medical evacuation. The patrol leader checklist, for example, mandated that soldiers obtain a clear statement of mission from their commanding officer before embarking on the patrol, identify not only a primary route but also a backup itinerary in case of hostile fire, and coordinate in advance with those who might be called upon to provide air or artillery support. Army officers created a website to compile and share a host of such leadership principles from those serving on the front lines.[19]

Firefighting

US wildland firefighting services have generated a set of checklists for teams working to suppress forest, grass, and other fires in the wilderness. One checklist requires that incident commanders have affirmative responses to three questions before launching a fire attack: Are controls in place for identifiable hazards? Are the planned tactics suitable given the anticipated fire behavior? Have unambiguous instructions been given to and understood by the firefighters? Similarly, the New York City Fire Department provides 13 checklists for officers responsible for major incidents, including a "Mayday Checklist" that requires ordering all unrelated two-way radio traffic to cease, establishing a staging area, and enlisting chaplains as needed.[20]

Selling

Two sales managers for Microsoft drew on a pilot's preflight checklist to create a presales checklist, asking before a sales call that their representatives web-search all who are expected at the meeting, commit their two-minute opening pitch to memory, and learn in detail about the personalities and politics of the firm during the engagement.[21]

Mission-specific checklists are also essential for leading laterally with peers and partners, and upwardly with superiors and executives.[22]

Chapter 4

Testing the Checklist

Taken together, the core and customized leader's checklists form a useful foundation for managers. But in a dynamic world, the principles always remain subject to change and improvement through recurrent testing and frequent refinement. Careful evaluation of the leadership principles can even call at times for a surprising rewiring.

Human resource managers at Google, for example, had anticipated that possessing technology expertise would be an important principle for leading at the company. Yet after testing what proved most effective with employees, Google researchers found that seven other leadership abilities had greater impact, including a capacity to articulate a strategy and to foster others' career development.[23]

In a study of the leadership at a major division of a large financial services firm, two fellow researchers and I uncovered the need for a similar revision in the customized checklist principles deemed to be most vital at that firm. One of our colleagues interviewed virtually all the top executives of a 4,000-person division, and from those interviews he identified 200 distinct capacities that at least some bankers viewed as invaluable for leading the operation. When he then asked the division leaders to rank the 200 capacities, the banking executives consistently placed 39 of them at the top.

Our colleague then took two additional testing steps that resulted in a surprising reconfiguration of the leader's checklist for this division. He first asked the leaders' peers, direct reports, and superiors to rate each of the division's leading bankers on those 39 capacities.

Next, he looked at the financial results of the leaders a year later, knowing that their performance depended much upon whether they could muster and align the energy of the bankers who reported to them.

With this data in hand, we found that only 9 of the 39 identified leadership capacities had a significant impact on the financial performance of the banking leaders. Qualities that were once highly rated, such as demonstrating strong commitment to company success, establishing a team-based sales culture, and streamlining the sales process, fell away when this baseline financial test was applied. Not surprisingly, the bank division subsequently focused its leadership development programs on a customized leader's checklist that comprised the nine principles that did make a difference—including the personal mentoring and motivating of the front-line bankers—but not the other 30 principles, a radical reconfiguring from what the bank had initially expected.[24]

Systematic study does not always confirm the status quo or even what is intuitively accepted. Sometimes, an analytic look upends or alters conventional, perhaps outdated wisdom. Testing the leader's checklist can thus be invaluable not only for confirming its principles but also for evolving them.

Chapter 5

Applying the Checklist

Would you have surgery performed by a doctor who failed to confirm the right patient was in the operating room and the correct procedure that he or she was to undertake? Are you willing to fly with a pilot who failed to check wind speed, flight plan, jet fuel, and other essential ingredients for ensuring a successful takeoff and landing?

You obviously would not. Many medical centers as a result require physicians to run through a specific checklist before commencing surgery. Aviation authorities around the globe require the same of pilots before takeoff. Indeed, in many newer jetliners, a commercial pilot is not given full access to the controls until the checklist has been electronically confirmed. To be sure, mistakes are still made in the operating room and on the runway, sometimes horrible ones—but because every item on the checklist is critical, mandating them all is a sensible effort to prevent missing any, as Atul Gawande's *The Checklist Manifesto* and research have made clear.[25]

Business leadership checklists are thus akin to professional leadership checklists already found in many arenas where they have long served as forceful guidelines for attention and action in high-performance endeavors. As in aviation and surgery, business leadership checklists imply that each of their itemized actions is mission critical for the user—and also that all the mission-critical actions for the user are contained on the list. A failure to address any single action on the list—such as checking aircraft fuel, confirming patient identity, or making decisions decisively—can thus lead to catastrophic failure even if all the other strictures have been observed. Users' reconfirmation of each of the checklist items thus helps ensure safe flights, successful surgery, and company results.

In extending the checklist concept to company managers and executives, how surprising it is, then, that those in leadership positions often fail to require the equivalent of themselves. We take for granted a pilot's thoroughness, or a surgeon's assiduousness, but we too often give ourselves a pass on adhering to an analogous list, or having one to check, even if we are facing fateful moments when a complete leadership inventory might be essential for sensibly directing or even saving an enterprise.

If executive compensation could somehow be linked both to creating a personalized leader's checklist *and* routinely applying it—in the same way pilots have to move through a preflight checklist before being allowed to take off—I believe that there would be far fewer midcareer crashes in the corporate arena. But with no authority or device insisting on a leader's checklist and its consistent application, enterprising managers are obliged to write their own and enforce their own compliance.

For application to occur, however, managers must work to overcome a host of predictable but preventable behavioral lapses. One of the most important is knowing what should be done but then failing to follow through, what researchers Jeffrey Pfeffer and Robert Sutton have termed the "knowing-doing gap." Even the best checklist has no value unless it is routinely activated to guide a leader's behavior.[26]

Doing so for most managers is an acquired rather than a natural skill. Drawing on both academic research and interviews with organizational leaders, I have found that managers fruitfully engage in four learning avenues that help them activate and apply their leader's checklist on a regular basis (see box 5.1).

Box 5.1. Mastering the Leader's Checklist

1. Study others' leadership moments.
2. Solicit coaching and mentoring.
3. Accept stretch experiences.
4. Conduct after-action reviews of personal leadership moments.

1. Study Others' Leadership Moments

A first step for learning to apply the leader's checklist is to become a self-directed student of leadership. This study can take many forms: reading leaders' biographies, witnessing leaders in action, and joining leadership development programs. What's critical is witnessing how others have worked with a full checklist or sometimes fallen short, often a powerful reminder to examine whether you are employing all the necessary principles.[27]

In my leadership development programs, for instance, I often draw upon the experience of teams of firefighters whose commanders invited disaster by employing a less-than-full checklist. I also frequently draw on an illustration from the pharmaceutical industry, one of the most informative moments I have ever studied for what it reveals about the value of a leader's checklist.[28]

Roy Vagelos, the director of research and development (R&D) at Merck, the giant US-based pharmaceutical company, faced a critical decision. A scientist, William Campbell, proposed developing a drug to combat a disease called river blindness. Hundreds of thousands had already lost their eyesight from the disease, and 20 million were at risk. Because the new treatment would be based on modification of an existing Merck product, a decision to invest might seem obvious— were it not for the fact that most of the victims lived in rural Nigeria and other poverty-stricken areas of West Africa. They could simply not afford the drug if it were developed, whatever its sight-saving powers. Even more worrisome for Merck as a commercial enterprise was the fact that if it created a cure, it was likely to find itself pressured to pay for its manufacturing and distribution to millions of victims living in some of the remotest regions of Africa.[29]

This might seem like a nonstarter for anybody with responsibility for the near-term performance of a publicly traded company. But quarterly and annual returns were only one of the R&D director's priorities. He also required long-term strategic thinking on behalf of the company, and that focused his attention on building income streams for years in the future. That line of thinking led him to conclude that although Merck might have to give the drug away once it was developed, the company would ultimately gain. Given a strengthened reputation among doctors and regulators, renewed ability to recruit top scientists, and greater brand recognition in countries like Nigeria, where Merck would long be remembered for its generosity, the company could more than make up for its immediate losses in producing a drug that no customers could afford.

With a balanced focus on both short-term returns and long-term gains as part of the checklist principle of strategic thinking, the director of R&D decided to invest in the sight-saving product. And while it was indeed costly in the near term, it proved providential over the decades. When the company sought scientists for its R&D operation years later, the fact that it had combated river blindness at its own expense proved a powerful recruitment tool. Attracting talent was further enabled when the scientist who had led the product's development, Campbell, received the Nobel Prize in Medicine.[30]

Merck's seeming "loss-leader" decision also helped make it a consistent winner in *Fortune* magazine's annual listing of the United States' most admired companies. And in the future, a significant portion of Nigeria's more than 200 million people might well give preference to Merck's products over those of rivals because of the cure's free distribution to some 10 million of their compatriots exposed to river blindness. Although Merck executives did not explicitly follow a leader's checklist at the time, the company's success demonstrates the effectiveness of an ordered, principles-based application of company leadership.

The same was true in the mid-2010s for CVS, the American pharmacy and convenience chain with thousands of stores across the United States. Its chief executive, Larry Merlo, had been vexed by the fact that his increasingly health-oriented enterprise still stocked cigarettes on its shelves. The company was already a $178 billion-a-year behemoth, but the CEO concluded that its continued growth as a healthcare provider was contradicted by the presence of tobacco products in its outlets. Hospital representatives wondered how CVS could proclaim its healthcare agenda while still selling cigarettes. The company's own medical officer questioned the pernicious impact of tobacco on customer health. CVS clinic nurses complained of the cigarette cartons behind their store's checkout counters.[31]

When a task force Merlo formed articulated the firm's long-term vision for itself—helping "people on their path to better health"—tobacco sales looked all that more hypocritical. Though tobacco products' elimination would be a financially costly short-term move, CVS's governing board embraced a proposal by Merlo to eliminate all such products from the company's 7,600 pharmacies.

As anticipated, the withdrawal did devastate the firm's short-term financial performance, costing CVS $2 billion in annual revenue and resulting in an immediate 7% drop in its stock price. But First Lady Michelle Obama gave the company a "thumbs-up" for its decision, and the president of an antismoking campaign extolled the move, saying, "This is truly an example of a corporation leading and setting a new standard." In markets where CVS ceased tobacco sales, 95 million fewer cigarette packs were sold during the first eight months. CVS later also removed trans fats from its private-label food, placed healthier products at the front of its stores, and added labels to its shelves denoting products as "heart-healthy" or "gluten-free." CVS stock had been trading at $73 a share at the time of the decision; despite the immediate stock-price dip, shares traded at $100 a year after the tobacco withdrawal.

Like Merck, CVS's principle-based action proved costly in the near term for the company's revenue, but it proved beneficial for its customers' health and the firm's reputation. Here, too, the chief executive did not explicitly draw on a leader's checklist, but Merlo's actions had again been guided by the kinds of leadership precepts that populate such a template.

2. Solicit Coaching and Mentoring

Solicit personal feedback from individuals who can provide informed, fine-grained advice on not only the leadership capacities that you already exhibit but also those principles that require more prominent display. It is hard to correct what you do not know you are not doing.[32]

3. Accept Stretch Experiences

Ask for and accept new responsibilities outside your comfort zone. By testing fresh territories and experiencing the setbacks they can bring, you can grow to appreciate the shortfalls in your own leader's checklist even as you learn to more consistently apply it. The absence of strategic thinking and honoring the room, for example, are not so evident in the early years of a career, but the diverse experiences that come with expanding responsibilities strengthen the felt need to apply such principles, especially after one has personally witnessed the costs of not doing so.

4. Conduct After-Action Reviews of Personal Leadership Moments

Transform a chilling experience into a learning opportunity. We often learn as much from setbacks as successes—sometimes even more from setbacks than successes—and with unflinching study of the stumbles, you should have a greater readiness to apply your leader's checklist the next time you are required to do so. This is partly why Cisco Systems' John Chambers had been one of the longest surviving chief executives in Silicon Valley, holding the company's reins for two decades. Chambers took the Cisco helm in 1995 and rode the internet wave in the late 1990s to make his company one of the world's most valued entities, with a market capitalization soaring above $500 billion. But when the internet bubble burst at the end of that decade, Cisco flipped from extraordinary growth to stunning contraction. Chambers and Cisco survived the collapse, and Chambers attributed much of the company's success in the decade that followed to what he learned when it felt as if he were touching the void.[33]

Chapter 6

Sustaining the Checklist

Organizational leadership has its greatest impact in times of uncertainty and change. When markets are predictable, when change is not in the offing, leaders can coast, at least for a while. It is when uncertainty becomes the norm and turbulence more commonplace that a leader's checklist becomes most consequential—a time, that is, much like the present.[34]

To prepare for such moments, we have thus far culled core leadership principles from informed observers, academic researchers, development programs, leaders' assessments, and program participants. In the process, we have found a core skill set that cuts across all venues—capacities such as thinking strategically, acting decisively, and communicating persuasively. Armed with these core precepts, we have also seen how customized principles are essential for leading specific organizations, playing distinct roles within them, running firms in varied national settings, and facing diverse market conditions—leadership of Indian companies, for example, requires greater emphasis on broad mission and social purpose than is common in the West. Finally, we looked at the need to customize the leader's checklist for an individual's immediate world. For a salesperson at Microsoft, additional principles were required that are distinct from those essential for a firefighter on 9/11.

With the creation of both core and mission-specific checklists, systematic testing and frequent revision are the essential next steps. As we had seen in the case of one financial services corporation, many of the leadership principles that its senior bankers thought vital proved to have little impact when carefully studied—but a small subset did, in fact, result in measurable leadership impact.

Appreciating the value of a leader's checklist is, of course, no guarantee that the checklist will be applied. To close the critical knowing-doing gap, four learning avenues prove valuable: self-directed study of leadership moments, coaching and mentoring, stretch experiences, and after-action review of personal leadership moments. By engaging in this multipronged approach, readers will be readier to apply their own templates at moments of uncertainty and change when their leadership really counts.

To be sustainable, however, a leader's checklist needs to be dynamic and adaptable, not static or fixed—constantly updated to reflect new situations and accumulated wisdom. With repeated study of experiences such as AIG's failure and the successful Chilean rescue operation, a leader's checklist should become progressively more grounded in evidence and more complete in coverage.

A checklist for leaders is certainly no substitute for comprehension and judgment, any more than the pilot's or surgeon's checklist is for flying a plane or operating on a patient. It is just intended to be a prompt, and for that purpose, simplicity and completeness are essential. So too is a personal commitment to generate and apply the principles at a time when they will especially make the difference.

PART II

The Leader's Checklist in Action

Chapter 7

Leadership Failure

What happens when there is no leader's checklist, or no attempt to apply one? Sometimes, very little. As every manager learns with cathartic relief, there are times when muddling through works just fine. But the higher the stakes, the more dire the consequences if a leader goes into a moment underprepared—and the muddling falls short.

For graphic illustration, American International Group's financial meltdown during the global financial crisis is hard to top. Under the leadership of just three chief executives since its founding in 1919, AIG had by 2007 become one of the world's most successful companies. With more than 100,000 employees and annual revenue exceeding $100 billion, the company ranked 10th on the Fortune 500 list, ahead of Goldman Sachs and not far behind Citigroup. AIG had become one of the 30 blue-chip companies that defined the Dow Jones Industrial Average.

A key driver of AIG's ascent had been one of its newer and smaller divisions, Financial Products (AIGFP). AIG's chief executive created the division in 1987 in response to rising demand for protection against debt defaults. Other financial institutions had been rapidly expanding their debt holdings, and AIGFP stepped forward to write insurance against their failure. Customers were promised that AIG would make them whole on defaults in securities ranging from auto loans and credit card receivables to subprime mortgages and credit default obligations.

At the outset, AIGFP charged relatively modest fees—in some cases just 0.02 cent per year for each dollar of insured risk—but across billions of dollars in such policies, it proved to be a lucrative business. Slow to grow at first, Financial Products accounted for only 4% of AIG's operating income by 1999, a dozen years after its launch. Over the next six years, though, AIGFP's share of the parent company's operating income soared to 17 percent. With fewer than 400 employees, AIGFP eventually came to back more than $1.5 trillion in credit default obligations, including some $58 billion in mortgage-backed securities—in all, the equivalent of well over half the GDP of France.[35]

The rapid growth in AIGFP earnings appeared to come with just modest risk to the company. AIG's chief executive reported to a group of investors in 2007 that the firm's risk metrics were "very reliable" and that they provided management with "a very high level of comfort." The head of AIGFP affirmed that promise: "We believe this is a money-good portfolio," and "The models we use are simple, they're specific and they're highly conservative." Enterprise risks, he added, were acceptable: "It is hard for us, without being flippant, to even see a scenario within any kind of realm of reason that would see us losing one dollar in any of those transactions."[36]

As they built the business, AIGFP executives learned that they could back large portfolios of debt at competitive rates in part because their parent held an AAA credit rating, the highest grade. Bestowed on just a handful of firms, it proved an invaluable advantage. Under the prevailing practice at the time, AIGFP was not obligated to set aside cash or assets to back its obligations because of its AAA status. If any of the insured debt defaulted, the company would of course have to pay its customers, but, using historical data, executives calculated that they could readily muster the cash that would be required to cover the relatively small number of losses expected at any given time. The AAA rating assured customers that AIG could indeed meet those obligations.

That calculus, however, proved lethal. After investment bank Lehman Brothers failed, institutional investors and rating agencies turned to see if other companies held great amounts of the toxic sub-prime mortgages that had pushed Lehman over the edge. AIGFP did, and on September 15, 2008, a major ratings agency dropped AIG's rating to A-minus. Because of the industry convention of requiring collateral if an insurer was rated A or below, the downgrade instigated massive collateral calls from AIGFP's customers—some $18 billion in just hours after Lehman's collapse, including those from banking heavyweights such as Barclays, Deutsche Bank, and Goldman Sachs.[37]

Investors rushed to sell their AIG shares, sending the company's stock plummeting by 60% in one day. The resulting credit panic brought on a requirement that AIGFP post still another $15 billion. To cover the mushrooming demands for collateral, AIG was forced to draw $28 billion on September 17 from an emergency fund created the night before. Further losses followed: $32 billion by the end of September and another $61 billion by end of the year, the largest annual shortfall in corporate history. In response, the US government injected more than $170 billion to save the firm and assumed control of nearly 80% of its voting shares.

How to explain such a spectacular collapse? Historically adverse market forces were certainly a factor, as were unusually good times before that. With the long-serving Maurice Greenberg at the helm until 2005, the firm had repeatedly found advantage in entering risky markets worldwide where others dared not tread, insuring everything from Russian trade to Nigerian oil. Strategic resourcefulness and audacious expansion had helped the company ascend to the Dow 30 and Fortune 10. But it is the duty of top management to anticipate bad times as well as good ones, and that is precisely where a thorough leader's checklist could have prevented, or at least drastically cushioned, AIG's fall.

Greenberg and his successor, for example, had extended the London-based Financial Products division a leash that proved far too lengthy, especially in light of how the division's aggressive instincts had already been blessed by AIG's executives and board. AIGFP employees reported that their division president received relatively little oversight from the company CEO and that the chief executive in turn received scant oversight from the directors. The board's limited vigilance in turn may have stemmed from AIG's relatively weak governance at the time. Not long before the fall, a governance-rating agency had given AIG governance a nearly failing grade of D.[38]

Company leaders had been repeatedly warned of the exceptional risks that the Financial Products division was taking. One federal regulator, for example, reported to the AIG governing board that it had found "weaknesses in AIGFP's documentation of complex structures transactions, in policies and procedures regarding account-ing, in stress testing, in communication of risk tolerances, and in the company's outline of lines of authority, credit risk management and measurement." Regulators warned of mounting subprime mortgage dangers and insisted that the board improve AIGFP's internal con-trols. AIG's outside auditor found fault with a host of its accounting practices.[39]

In hindsight, it is easy to understand why the company CEO and division president paid so little attention to admonitions from regu-lators, auditors, and increasingly the market itself. AIGFP was a shooting star whose rapid expansion contributed mightily to its par-ent company's results and ensured annual bonuses across the board. We know from academic studies that company success can result in excessive confidence and risk-taking, and we know from human nature that we are loath to look a gift horse in the mouth. What's more, robust growth can lead to unrealistic appraisals of latent risks, particularly low-probability, high-impact threats that can prove catastrophic.[40]

Yet, since this is, in fact, a clearly marked and predictable path of human behavior, one of the obligations of AIG's leadership was to recognize such behavioral shortcomings *before* they could wreak havoc on the enterprise. If the AIGFP president was not heeding the warning signs of excessive risk, that responsibility fell to his boss, the AIG chief executive. And if the chief executive was unable to foresee the gathering storm, the board was duty-bound to guard against his overoptimism. Intervention at any one of these levels might have helped prevent a catastrophe of historic proportions. The absence of such intervention at every level virtually assured it.

The 13th principle of *The Leader's Checklist* is readily drawn from this account. It helps leaders see beyond the momentary euphoria of flush times so they can concentrate on steering an enterprise through both the prosperous and the hard times ahead.

---

13. **Dampen Overoptimism and Excessive Pessimism.**
    Counter the hubris of success, focus attention on latent threats and unresolved problems, and protect against taking unwarranted risks; at the same time, bolster confidence in coming back from downturns and setbacks.

Chapter 8

Leadership Triumph

If AIG's collapse is a story of unmitigated disaster, the 2010 rescue of 33 trapped Chilean miners is its polar opposite, a tale of unalloyed success. Regardless of outcome, I believe that close study of leadership at its worst and at its best is an essential source of fresh insights into what is essential for a complete leader's checklist, and the miners' rescue in Chile is certainly among the finest examples available in recent years. It reinforces the value of the consistent use of the template for guiding action—and it underscores still another principle for the leader's checklist.[41]

Laurence Golborne made his mark as chief executive of Chile's largest retail chain, Cencosud, an enterprise with more than 10,000 employees and annual turnover of $10 billion. In early 2010, the newly elected president of Chile, Sebastián Piñera, asked Golborne to serve with him as the nation's mining minister, and they took office together on March 11, 2010.[42]

Though he had initially questioned whether he should accept the government ministry in the absence of any prior experience in the industry, Golborne believed that his management know-how would more than make up for the lack of technical grounding. The mining ministry is "where I can contribute my management skills," he explained to his family. And now, without miner-rescue experience either, he would nonetheless conclude that his management capacities were enough for him to assume responsibility for rescuing the 33 miners trapped in the Atacama. "Although I do not come from the mining world," Golborne explained, "and was questioning myself what I could do in the mine—how I could help in the rescue given the magnitude of the problem—I understood I had to be there." But getting to that point entailed a wrenching encounter.[43]

Golborne arrived at the San José mine, the scene of the disaster, two days after the cave-in, uncertain about the role he should play but determined to see the situation for himself. Later that same day, a rescue team returned from the depths and reported that the entire mine had become so unstable that nobody could safely enter most of it for any reason, let alone descending all the way to the stranded miners some 2,000 feet below. A member of the rescue squad confided to the mining minister, "They must be dead," and "if they are not dead, they will die."

In the interest of transparency, Golborne decided to immediately disclose the bleak appraisal to the miners' relatives who had converged at the mine's entry. But when he noticed two daughters of one of the trapped miners weeping after he reported the dispiriting assessment, he lost his own composure and for a moment could not continue. "Minister, you cannot break down," shouted one of the relatives. "You have to give us strength!" For Golborne, it became a turning point. The meeting with the miners' families ended his ambivalence about whether he and the government of Chile should assume direct authority over the rescue, even though the accident had occurred at a privately owned mine—and despite the fact that the nation's top mining official had never assumed full responsibility for a mining rescue in the past.

Taking direct control, Golborne decided to initiate a plan to drill five-inch boreholes to locate the miners. The miners' precise location was unknown, and such drilling normally required a tolerance for a seven-degree variance in alignment, more than enough to miss the miners' refuge even if its location had been pinpointed. Though he had trained as an engineer before going into retail, Golborne quickly saw that the engineering challenges inherent in the rescue attempts went far beyond his own proficiencies. "I realized that in the technical issues we did not have the needed leadership," he confessed. "I could not provide that leadership. Although I am an engineer, I do not have any technical knowledge about mining."

With volunteers flooding onto the site—some 20 organizations were soon offering their services—a range of other rescue proposals began to emerge. To cope with the flow, Golborne set out to assemble a band of specialists, starting with an experienced engineer from Chile's state-owned copper company who brought both the know-how and credibility required. "There were too many voices," Golborne complained, "and nobody at the site seemed to have the leverage to cut the cake." When the specialist arrived at the San José site, Golborne was unequivocal about the role that the engineer must play: "You have to take charge!"

Working with the miners' families became a separate challenge, as they forcefully pressed for regular updates and, above all, speedy extraction. "We're not going to abandon this camp," declared one of their spokespersons, "until we go out with the last miner left!" Their skepticism ran deep, and emotions ran high. Banners proclaiming "Daddy, we are waiting for you" and "Son, we are here" waved over the families' camp. To another specialist, a psychologist and safety director for one of the state-owned mines, Golborne delegated responsibility for working with both the miners' relatives and the many organizations that had arrived to assist.

The government itself was a separate and problematic constituency. Many officials questioned the wisdom of committing the state to an effort that could well end in tragedy. The mine's owners would bear most of the onus for a disastrous outcome if Golborne did not become engaged, but once he had committed, the state would inevitably share or even take the bulk of the blame. To overcome the lingering risk aversion among Santiago officials, and also to mobilize the government to secure counsel and equipment from around the world, Golborne handed the assignment off to a well-connected insider, the cabinet chief for Chile's Ministry of the Interior.

Further consolidating his team, Golborne removed the mine's owner from any role in the rescue. And he worked to ensure both personal equanimity and single-mindedness among the small band of leaders he had formed—equanimity because of the intense demands, riveting focus because of the human stakes. But with his top team in place, he then faced a question on his own decision-making: Should he take a role in the life-and-death decisions ahead, or should he leave them to the experts on his team? He worried that the decisions could go wrong without his involvement, yet he also feared reactions if he made the final decisions but the rescue later faltered or failed. He feared others would later ask why he had gotten in the middle of it if he knew so little about it.

Golborne decided to fall back on the management methods that had served him and his business well in the past. He asked for guidance and the rationale for technical proposals coming from his team but did not shrink from direct engagement in their final resolution. "I did what I normally do," he explained, and that was to "let the experts talk." And he made sure that his direct reports had compelling reasons for their strategies before they executed them. "With my style," he said, "I started asking questions," but he reserved for himself the final authority for making the decisions.

Underscoring and heightening all of Golborne's actions was the race against time. He assumed that any of the miners who survived the cave-in would have virtually no food, and he worried about life-threatening injuries among those who had not perished. The mining minister accordingly adopted a strategy of redundancy, seeking to reach and then extract the miners through simultaneous parallel measures. The drilling began with no fewer than 10 five-inch boreholes to locate the miners, and one finally paid off: 15 days after the cave-in, a drill pierced the small cavity where the miners had taken refuge. When the drill head was withdrawn to the surface, taped to it was a message in red letters, "Estamos Bien En El Refugio los 33" (We are fine in the shelter, the 33). For families, it was a moment of jubilation; for Golborne, a personal epiphany and turning point.

Golborne and his team immediately focused on the obvious next task, extracting the miners. They had already vetted some 10 different plans, and their attention converged on three that would open person-sized shafts all the way to the miners' refuge. Each entailed a different approach, and because it was still a race against the clock, Golborne authorized all three to proceed at the same time.

Thirty-three days later, one of the three plans, viewed skeptically by some of the engineers at the outset, succeeded before the others. One by one, the miners were transported to the surface in a thin, cable-drawn capsule, and on October 13, the shift supervisor—the last of the miners to be raised—emerged to greet his son and report to the Chilean president, who had joined Golborne for the crowning moment, "I've delivered to you this shift of workers, as we agreed I would."

President Piñera replied, "I gladly receive your shift because you completed your duty, leaving last like a good captain," adding, "You are not the same after this, and Chile won't be the same either." A group of rescuers who were still in the refuge after the last miner ascended displayed a sign seen by millions of television viewers around the world: "Misión Cumplida Chile."

The rescue required that Golborne use virtually all the leader's checklist principles identified so far. He thought strategically, conveyed his character, honored the room, motivated the troops, embraced the front lines, and critically took charge even without a formal brief to do so because he had the management experience to handle the job and was optimally positioned for the task.

Like the disastrous AIG experience, though, the victorious Chilean one also points to still another checklist principle: the value of building a top team diverse in capabilities and experience.

---

14. **Build a Diverse Top Team.** Leaders need to take final responsibility, but leadership is also a team sport best played with an able and diversified roster of those collectively capable of resolving the key challenges.

Golborne's experience also fleshes out still another checklist principle. He stressed the need to repeatedly remind his rescue team of the "dream," the ultimate purpose of the hard and often tedious work that is the substance of success. "You have to be positive" about the challenge, he said. "You have to be optimistic." And for instilling that determination to succeed, you have "to be with the guys" and "to face them with faith that you are going to be able to solve it."

---

7. **Motivate the Workforce.** Appreciate the distinctive intentions that people bring, and then build on those varied motives to draw the best from each.

Golborne added another principle not contained in the checklist above, though it perhaps should have been: the overwhelming importance of sustenance from above. From the first moment of the crisis, Chilean president Sebastián Piñera put himself foursquare behind the rescue initiative. "President Piñera committed that we would, with all our effort, find them," Golborne recalled. "At that moment, I felt empowered to take control."

Forcefully committing the country to the rescue, Golborne said, "was key for the success of this operation." And though the initiative did not seem assured of any success at the outset, the president's unswerving support proved essential for first locating the miners—"one of the best moments in my life," Golborne told me—and then raising them to the surface.[44]

Chapter 9

Missing in Action

While the *Leader's Checklist* is defined by 16 principles, multiple managers have let me know that, in their experience, three of those principles have more often been missing in action than others. In some cases, the managers said, they had too seldom or inconsistently utilized them in the exercise of their own leadership. Just as often, they had too infrequently witnessed their use among other leaders, including their superiors, who should have embraced them. Either way, the result has been the same: compromised leadership at a moment when an enterprise cannot afford to flounder.

The three principles that many managers have found most lacking in themselves and others:

---

3. **Honor the Room.** Expressing confidence in and support for those who work for you.

6. **Communicate Persuasively.** Communicating in ways that people will never forget.

15. **Place Common Interest First.** Stressing common purpose first, parochial concern last.

A compelling affirmation of the power the 15th principle, placing common interest first, could be seen at the White House on November 16, 2010, when President Barack Obama presented the

Medal of Honor to Army Staff Sergeant Salvatore A. Giunta. During the sergeant's second combat tour in Afghanistan, his team had been ambushed by a well-armed insurgent group. Giunta had raced forward under fire at great risk to himself to render aid to the wounded and to rescue an injured GI being dragged away by insurgents. The United States cited Giunta for his "unwavering courage, selflessness, and decisive leadership while under extreme enemy fire" and for his "extraordinary heroism and selflessness above and beyond the call of duty." When the president detailed this selfless act of leadership during the White House ceremony—with Giunta's wife and parents and the survivors of his unit present and the Medal of Honor recipient himself standing at the president's side—the East Room, according to one reporter, "was so silent you could hear a rustle from across the room."[45]

Why are these three principles honored more in the breach than in practice? I suspect the answer lies in the fact that so many management cultures do not adequately emphasize or build these mission-critical principles into their leadership development programs. Whatever the source of the shortfall, however, their absence is keenly felt and sometimes proves disastrous to company reputation, the bottom line, and even the national interest.

Think, for example, of the inability of then–BP chief executive Tony Hayward to communicate persuasively his concern for the environmental impact of his company's ruptured wellhead in the Gulf of Mexico, or of the ways in which so many members of the investment banking community appeared to put parochial self-interest ahead of investor and national interest during the global financial crisis.[46]

As for failing to honor the room, look no further than Jeff Kindler, the former CEO of one of the world's largest pharmaceutical companies, Pfizer. By many accounts, Kindler repeatedly confronted, interrogated, criticized, and micromanaged his top managers, even publicly upbraiding a board member. With little real followership in the wake of his consistent failure to honor any room and with negative share performance to show for his efforts, Kindler was bounced by the board less than five years after taking office.[47]

Chapter 10

Challenging Times

While all principles should be applicable to most moments when leadership is on the line, several take on special salience when facing especially stressful or troubling times. The COVID-19 pandemic and all the challenges surrounding it are one prominent example. Drawing on the freshly conveyed experience of managers in a host of settings, the checklist principles most vital for challenging times are the following:

---

2. **Think and Act Strategically.** Set forth a pragmatic strategy for moving forward both short- and long-term, and ensure that it is widely understood; consider all the players, and anticipate reactions and resistance before they are manifest.

4. **Take Charge and Lead Change.** Embrace a bias for action, taking responsibility even if it is not fully or formally delegated, particularly if you are well positioned to make a difference.

5. **Act Decisively.** Make good and timely decisions, and ensure that they are executed.

There is no more important time for leaders to remember to highlight these principles in action than when a company is restructuring, a community is struggling, or a country is floundering.

With wild gyrations on the world's stock markets, downgrades and even threatened defaults in sovereign debt, national shutdowns in the face of contagions, and sputtering recoveries in national economies, enterprise leaders are all but compelled to double down on strategic thinking, decisive decision-making, and a willingness to take direct charge.

Imagine, for example, a United States is which business leaders took greater charge of boosting employment, reducing inequality, increasing diversity, and protecting elections. With the chance of comprehensive Washington intercession for some of these issues close to nil given the nation's political gridlock, businesses could make them a company priority—and doing so would require their leaders to build on the tripartite principles of strategic thinking, taking charge, and acting decisively.

Yes, many of the institutional investors that now control two-thirds of America's publicly traded shares might well take exception—their focus is on delivering near-term shareholder value above all else, while punishing executives and directors who repeatedly fall short. But what might seem an idée fixe of the American way is really a moment's artifice, a prescription that served a past era but less well the current one.[48]

If Fortune 500 companies, for instance, each added only 1,000 Americans to their payrolls, they could jointly expand US employment by a half million. Working together, an inner circle of leading executives, directors, and owners might commit to creating a million new US jobs within the next year or to establishing a research and development fund for innovative ways to expand employment and wages.

When it comes to growth in employment in the United States, a mobilized leadership of those who own and oversee the apex of the private sector could thus help provide it at a time when the country's political leaders might not. Or imagine their impact on public health if the chief executives of each required proof of vaccination against COVID-19 from all employees. To return to the principle in question, this would entail taking charge when others seemingly cannot.[49]

Crisis Moments

Throughout my academic study and my development work in leadership, I have looked at how others perform during crisis moments—nearby, across the globe, or through the long reach of time. Feedback from managers has shown this avenue of exploration to be of particular value, especially in a time of often-contradictory media messages. Crisis moments—not the network-television variety, but on-the-scene, first-person accounts of leadership during calamitous instants—often provide indelible insights about how to lead when we are called to lead, whatever the moment.

Many managers have informed me that they wish I had included more narratives of individuals whose leadership has been exceptionally instructive. I spoke with Joseph Pfeifer, then the Chief of Counterterrorism and Emergency Preparedness for the New York City Fire Department. Pfeifer brought extensive experience in leading others during both ordinary and extraordinary times. As a Citywide Command Chief, he served as incident commander for rescue services in the North Tower of the World Trade Center on September 11, 2001. He also led the development of the department's strategic plans and terrorism-preparedness strategy. My interview with him reinforces the checklist principles but also offers fresh insights into their application, especially the one that reads:

---

5. Act Decisively. Make good and timely decisions, and ensure that they are executed.

Pfeifer was conducting a routine check on a gas leak near the World Trade Center that morning when—at 8:46 a.m.—he heard the roar of a low-flying aircraft as it streaked overhead. Pfeifer looked up in time to see the aircraft smash into the center's North Tower, and judging by the angle and velocity of approach, he instantly concluded it was not an accident but a terrorist attack.[50]

"At that moment," Pfeifer said, "we knew we were going to the biggest fire of our lives," and he immediately radioed for a massive deployment of firefighters and beyond. He then directed the urgent rescue efforts in the main lobby of the North Tower, also known as Tower One, during the following hour, making dozens of rapid-fire decisions to effect rescue of those above. And in keeping with the leader's precept of acting decisively, when the nearby South Tower collapsed at 9:59 a.m., Pfeifer radioed a message to the many firefighters who were then high up bringing people down: "Command to all units in Tower One, evacuate the building!"

Our interview also points to two other issues that slipped somewhat beneath the radar in the first edition of *The Leader's Checklist*: the vital importance of having a personal stake in the game, and the critical value of not only taking charge and building a top team but also creating and coordinating a network of teams.

On the first point, Pfeifer describes a firefighter who tracked him down after a three-alarm blaze, simply to say, "Chief, I just want to let you know that I'll follow you down any hallway." As nice as the compliment was, Pfeifer realized that the firefighter was really saying that he was looking to Pfeifer to keep him safe when leading him into harm's way. Equally implicit was the knowledge that the firefighter trusted Pfeifer with his own well-being because he knew that Pfeifer had put his own life on the line in the past. Leadership is not just about giving direction from afar, Pfeifer observes; it is also "about sharing the danger," of having skin in the game, of appreciating personally what others are being asked to do and the risks they face.

On the second point, Pfeifer drew on the events of 9/11 to offer an affirmative message for any leader facing complex, fast-moving, and high-stakes events. Sharing intelligence among diverse parties about rapidly evolving conditions should be a prebuilt capacity, well in place before calamity strikes. Equally important for any leader is a readiness to guard against what Pfeifer terms "organizational bias"—in his world, where "firefighters go to firefighters, police go to police," and emergency medical personnel pull inward. What is needed is exactly the opposite. If "command and control" is a foundation for authoritative leadership, Pfeifer concludes from his experience in 9/11 and beyond, complex events require leaders who also "connect, collaborate, and coordinate."

Chapter 11

The 16th Principle
Think Like a CEO

Throughout this volume, I have stressed that most of the core principles presented here are applicable in most situations. The 16th principle, however, is applicable in all circumstances—a precept for action without which no leader's checklist should be considered complete.

Let's revisit a scene from the beginning of this volume—but before we get there, we will need to set the clock back to April 12, 1861. At 4:30 that morning, rebel forces in South Carolina opened fire on a federal fort in Charleston Harbor. The garrison commander gave up the fortress with no fatalities, and though a minor clash compared with what would follow, that opening salvo on Fort Sumter triggered a four-year civil war that would leave more than 700,000 dead.[51]

Among the hundreds of thousands to enlist included a Maine resident and Bowdoin College professor named Joshua Lawrence Chamberlain. Rising from lieutenant colonel to major general, he would see combat at the battles of Fredericksburg, Gettysburg, and Petersburg, and he was with the Union Army of the Potomac when Robert E. Lee's Army of Northern Virginia surrendered at Appomattox, Virginia, on April 9, 1865.

To mark the moment, General Ulysses S. Grant, who had accepted the formal surrender on behalf of the Union, ordered a follow-up ceremony for April 12, with more than 4,000 Union soldiers to be lined up at attention on one side of a field. Lee's defeated infantry units were then to march onto the field to place their regimental flags and firearms at the foot of a Union officer in charge. For the honor of orchestrating the event and overseeing it, Grant designated Chamberlain.

As the first Confederate brigade approached Union forces at the field on April 12, four years to the date since the rebel firing on Fort Sumter, Chamberlain ordered a bugle call that told Union soldiers to "carry arms"—a posture of respect in which soldiers hold the musket in their right hand with the muzzle perpendicular to their shoulders. Both Union and Confederate soldiers understood its meaning, since their military traditions had emanated from the same sources.

A Southern general riding near the front of the Confederate forces, John B. Gordon, appreciated the respectful signal that Chamberlain's soldiers displayed toward the rebel soldiers on their day of ignominy, and Gordon ordered the same posture to be returned by his own troops. As described by Chamberlain himself, "Gordon, at the head of the marching column, riding with heavy spirit and downcast face, catches the sound of the shifting arms, looks up, and, taking the meaning," instructed "his successive brigades to pass us with the same position."[52]

The incident became known as a "salute returning a salute," a moment remembered for years by those who witnessed or heard of it, and one that implied reconciliation. Some of Chamberlain's fellow officers were angered by witnessing such a fraternal act after battling the same soldiers on so many killing fields and for their advocacy of such heinous ends. And for Chamberlain himself, it was a matter of saluting those who had tried to kill him only two weeks earlier. In a skirmish on March 29, Confederate soldiers had wounded Chamberlain in the arm and chest. A year before that, they shot him through the hip and groin during the Union siege of Petersburg. In all, through 20 battles and numerous skirmishes during three years of service, Chamberlain had been wounded six times, and he would eventually succumb to the Petersburg injury.[53]

For President Abraham Lincoln, the South's capitulation at Appomattox constituted not only an ending point for the armed rebellion but also a starting point for national reconciliation. Even for him, however, the road to reunification was a bitter pill given the Union's grievous losses on the battlefields. Events would take a horrible personal turn just two days after Chamberlain's salute to the rebel army as the president and his wife attended a performance at Ford's Theatre in Washington.

For both sides, though, gestures of reconciliation were more important than the hostilities that remained. The latter were natural, the former learned, and Chamberlain's moment at the conclusion of the Civil War serves to remind us of the vital importance of the final principle: think like a company president or a company chief executive even though you are layers below them. This last checklist precept is expressed in our oft-used phrases of "servant" leadership, and in my experience it is one of most vital of all your leadership principles.

---

16. **Think Like a CEO.** In taking leadership actions at your level, work through what a company CEO or even a country president would expect of you at that moment, and bring that expectation into your actions.

Thinking Like a CEO Before You Get There

The 16th principle can also be seen in the promotion of ITT Corporation's chief financial officer to chief executive officer of one of the company's spin-offs. For her leadership of the latter, it was fortunate that she was thinking like a CEO well before she became its CEO.[54]

We all start our working life somewhere, and it can be a long climb to the top, with many rungs to be ascended. In business, it is the company specialist—whether in engineering, finance, or marketing—who is first invited onto that ladder. And only much later, when fast-tracking functional experts or divisional directors emerge as generalists, appreciating most of their company's roles and operations, do they have a shot at the highest rung where all functions and divisions merge into one.

This was Denise Ramos's pathway. She studied economics in college and finance in graduate school, and then rose through the financial ranks at energy, food, and furniture companies, ever upward but always with the same core function, culminating in her service as chief financial officer for the near-legendary ITT Corporation. "I always enjoyed numbers and how they related to the operations of the business," she recalled, and "that really informed how I thought." Yet, along the way, Ramos also learned to think beyond her specific sphere, appreciating that counting the cash was essential but not enough to know how to allocate it well. She came to consider how her firm's functions and divisions could work together, even if that bigger picture was not yet her official remit.

When ITT Corporation split itself into three new companies, its governing board concluded that its CFO was ready to run one of the spin-offs. Hers was still an incomplete résumé, but the directors believed that she would readily expand her range of expertise in the top job because she was already thinking much like a chief executive.

The moment came for Ramos to test her wings as the generalist-in-chief, the person ultimately responsible for every aspect of every decision, but the spin-off that the governing board assigned her was a mess. It carried asbestos liabilities, bumpy operations, and cobbled-together divisions. Though officially named ITT Inc., around the water cooler it was known as "Remain Co.," or sometimes just "else." So, in addition to the challenges of quickly rounding out her skill set beyond reporting year-end financial results, and on top of becoming proficient in ensuring that her workforce had the wherewithal to build and sell worldwide the desalination systems, shock absorbers, and water pumps that generated those results, Ramos faced the challenge of learning how to revamp the entire enterprise. She would have to streamline, connect, and build the many pieces into a coherent, freestanding company.

The board chair, Frank MacInnis, deemed Ramos prepared. He had always been impressed when she reported as CFO to the old ITT board, on which MacInnis had served. "I realized it was the kind of report that one would expect from a CEO," he said, meaning that, while Ramos did not yet have to make the final calls, she grasped their complexity. She had come in as a broad and deep long-term planner, MacInnis recalled, and she often seemed more on top of operating detail than even the CEO. She would report the firm's cash position at the moment, a CFO's stock-in-trade, but then she would also identify what ought to be done with the cash, in effect moving from company finance to business strategy, the province of the top executive.

To Ramos, this broader awareness came naturally. In a finance role, she explained, you do not have all the pieces that have to come together, but as chief executive it's required "that you give time to connect all the dots." Now at the summit of the entire enterprise, she appreciated that she would have to be much more focused on the company's strategy, its values, and its culture. And in contrast to her functional behind-the-scenes background, she came to recognize that she was now also the public face of the company.

MacInnis told Ramos that he and his fellow directors had picked her because she had already learned to appreciate the imperatives of the corner office. "You had always spoken as if you were running the company," he explained. Thus, MacInnis and the board believed that she would think and judge holistically even if she had long served in only one function, bringing the firm's disparate stovepipes together when reaching major decisions. But Ramos still thought long and hard about the offer. She recognized that she brought little direct familiarity with how to run manufacturing lines. "I knew this was my weak spot," she confessed. It was too late to acquire that experience now, but to tighten her strategic fit with the company's imperatives, she vowed to bring in operating veterans to complement her own skill set.

Adding to the challenges that Ramos faced in her first months as CEO, morale was terrible, dampened by the uncertainties of the breakup and the orphan stature of the "else." Doubts about job security and career pathways prevailed; even solvency was questioned.

She also knew that ITT 's new divisions shared little history or common identity—we "did not know who we were."

As if trying to figure out the personality of this new, smaller ITT were not a big enough challenge, Ramos also had to master the many nuances of her fresh, more elevated role at the company. "People pay attention to everything you say," and "I had to listen very carefully to everybody on my team." When "they have a problem, I have a problem, and I had to hear it in detail." She also came to better appreciate that no two of her new executives were the same. Each required customized direction. At the same time, she learned that it was best to have people in her inner circle who were different from one another—and different from her.

In all, Ramos spent five years working to establish the new ITT Inc.'s mission, reputation, identity, and brand, as well as its work habits, employee moods, and prevailing norms. She pulled divisions together, moved operations from one country to another, and streamlined the workforce. She had been very clear about the limitations of her past experience, and the dangers of a mismatch with her new requirement, when she was considering stepping up to become CEO. She had never wanted to project anything that was inauthentic or to adopt practices that were not true to herself. If "you bring in something not you," she warned, "people see it," and that would irreparably damage others' confidence in her.

Under Ramos's leadership, ITT navigated a precipitous drop in oil prices, reduced asbestos claims against it, and created a shared purpose and separate identity as a maker of engineered products for a range of private manufacturers and even public agencies. The company's annual revenue in 2018, the last year of Ramos's leadership, exceeded $2.7 billion, up from $1.9 billion the year before she became chief executive. From the first day of Ramos's service to the last, the value of the S&P 500 index rose 123%; the value of the new ITT had risen by 161%. "We believe outgoing CEO Denise Ramos," wrote one equity analyst near the end of her term, "can take much deserved credit for defying the skeptics."

The incomplete leadership résumé with which Ramos had arrived at the top did not stand in the way of creating value. She had already learned to think well beyond the finance function, and then she learned as well to pull all her divisions into a functioning whole. "You have to fit what the company wants at the moment," Ramos observed. She came in as her new enterprise was taking form, requiring a readiness to cajole, invent, and improvise; restructure and regularize; and explain the "Remain Co." strategy and even its very existence to skeptical customers and owners. In all, she had brought her earlier thinking like a CEO into her current service as the CEO, a mission-critical principle for leading when she stepped up to CEO.

PART III

Building Out Your Company Checklists

Chapter 12

The Team Leader's Checklist

The leader's checklist has been developed here for the individual performer, whether a company manager, hospital administrator, or community leader. Still, the leadership actions of teams, teams of teams, and governing boards are usefully framed and disciplined by the same kind of template, and from similar personal experience and university research we offer a set of additional checklists for navigating your way through the collective setting in which you and your teams and boards exercise your and their leadership as well.

We all work on many teams, and we are formally or informally contributing to the leadership of all. Drawing on a range of studies team leadership, box 12.1 displays a guide for team leadership.

The value of the team leader's checklist can be appreciated from the curvilinear relationship between stress and performance, as shown in box 12.1. To the left of the panic point for individuals and poorly led teams, the heightened adrenaline feed from increased stress concentrates the mind, mobilizes energy, and eliminates distractions. To the right of the panic point, however, we no longer think so clearly and are less able to reason carefully. Well-led teams, however, are better able to insulate themselves against that stress, thereby pushing the panic point to the right. With higher levels of stress, the quality of their decisions and performance improves rather than degrades. That is why the armed forces have long seen camaraderie

Box 12.1. Team Leader's Checklist

1. **Learn:** Strengthen the team both cognitively and affectively.
2. **Design well:** Set distinct goals with defined and varied tasks for team members.
3. **Build identity:** Share experience and strengthen camaraderie to create a set of norms and values.
4. **Dynamic:** As the market changes, evolve the team's expectations and tasks.
5. **Diverse and inclusive:** Optimize variety in the members' backgrounds and experiences, and engage all in the team's work and achievements.
6. **Size right:** Not too large, not too small.
7. **Set compelling direction, strong structure, supportive context, and shared mindset.** Create a team agenda, inner scaffolding, outer backing, and aligned thinking for members to row together in the right direction.[55]

Figure 12.1. Avoiding the Panic Point

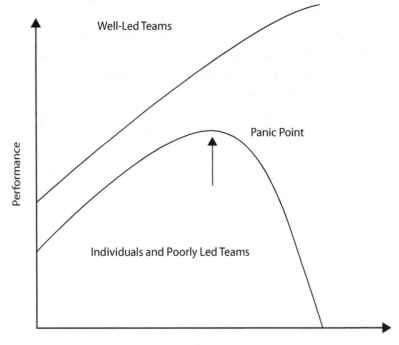

as an essential foundation for their primary fighting units. Equally, it is why so many companies have long invested in building and developing teams. When formed into well-led units, both combat and business teams are better able to make good and timely decisions in challenging and risky environments.[56]

Chapter 13

The Team of Teams' Checklist

I n *Team of Teams*, Stanley McChrystal reminds us that enterprises of almost any size run on teams of teams, where groups, divisions, offices, functions, and regions are pulled together by general managers who unite them but are not necessarily part of them. For this, we recommend a team of teams' checklist with two mission-critical components for uniting them.[57]

1. Create Culture: Foster a Common Mindset and Shared Mission Across Teams

In 2020–21, COVID-19 all but eliminated face-to-face contact of any kind. How could a company leader even begin to sustain purpose, direction, and energy with human interactions limited to Zoom? For leading remotely or when personal contact is limited by large numbers, company culture can be the vital medium for uniting teams across the enterprise.[58]

For illustration, we turn to Johnson & Johnson, which had already mastered the challenges of remote leadership through a deceptively simple means before the outbreak. Comprising a sprawling combination of consumer goods, pharmaceuticals, and medical devices, J&J offers everything from Band-Aids and pain relievers to infection medications and hip-replacement hardware, making it one of America's largest corporations, among the top 50 in the Fortune 500. It works through some 260 operating companies, and its annual revenue totals more than a third of $1 trillion. But the firm has also faced its share of billion-dollar recalls and penalties for faulty or allegedly harmful insulin cartridges, birth control pills, implantable stents, opioid tablets, and even talcum powder.

Many decades after its founding in 1886, as the company expanded and took on more and more employees, its executives had supplemented their face-to-face leadership with a written credo articulating the company's values. In some 300 words, the credo stressed the company's commitment to its consumers, employees, and community—and not just its stockholders. The terse avowal of enterprise purpose was intended to guide all employees without the company's leaders having to directly instruct them individually. The resulting declaration has since become one of J&J's trademarks, a tightly phrased expression of company ideals that everybody is asked to share, a kind of universal template for guiding their behavior within the corporate sphere, uniting thousands of teams in common resolve.

Though a number of companies circulate credo-like statements, over its history J&J has stressed its creed more than most, applying and reinforcing it repeatedly. In effect it created a vehicle for leveraging the chief executive's leadership across the firm, communicating what the CEO wants all teams to know without his having to personally convey it to any. But while a credo can guide a firm's culture for years—at J&J it is set in stone—its language can also fall behind the times and impair its impact.

When Alex Gorsky, Johnson & Johnson's seventh chief executive, took charge in 2012, he came to believe that the written guidance he'd inherited had indeed become dusty, its words and phrases antiquated, its impact enervated. He would somehow have to update and modernize it if it was to leverage his leadership, but he would also have to tread carefully.

Johnson & Johnson's market had become more global, its customers more diverse, its employees more purposeful, and litigation more damaging. Looking at younger generations in the ranks—Gen X and millennials—Gorsky found that they "want to be part of something bigger than themselves."

And to him, the credo's words seemed less resonant, some of its edicts no longer clear, others no longer appropriate. The credo had aligned thousands during an earlier Tylenol-poisoning and recall crisis, but in Gorsky's view its power for doing so in a future crisis—perhaps a virus pandemic—was perceptibly waning. Still, it had served as the company's inertial guidance for some 75 years, most of it was still relevant, and the cost to his stature of wrongly amending it would be high.

After privately pondering the possibility and the risks for several years, Gorsky finally raised the revision question with his top team, the company's executive committee with a dozen heads of his operating divisions and company functions, including consumer products, medical devices, pharmaceuticals, human resources, supply chains, and finance. These were the officers through whom his leadership was directly exercised, and their active acceptance of a revision would be a sine qua non for its execution.

The executive committee's initial reaction confirmed Gorsky's cautionary reluctance. Some members were for updating the credo in principle, but they needed to see what was proposed. Others opposed any modification on principle. Why change the wording, some said, when the company was doing well and thus, by implication, was well served by the current credo?

Undaunted, Gorsky brought forward a marked-up version of the credo for the executive committee's review. And after several months of rumination and a final weekend redrafting at home, Gorsky presented a revised version of the credo to his executive committee and the governing board for a final vetting. The final approval, however, would be his alone.

Gorsky's changes elevated patients first among company responsibilities, now ahead of doctors and nurses; focused the company on strategy, not just cost cutting; called for purpose in work, not just job security; added diversity to workplace dignity; pressed for "capable leaders" in place of "competent management"; added public health as a priority; and stressed research and innovation for the long haul.

The chief executive's subsequent leadership challenge was to communicate the revised credo to the company's employees so that it would stick; otherwise, it would remain just empty rhetoric. He introduced his new version of the company's values during a private telecast to the entire J&J workforce of more than 100,000. Gorsky asked that every manager meet monthly with his or her direct reports on the implications of the new credo for their own actions. Symptomatic of the high stakes and leadership significance, the chief executive's voice broke at several points during the presentation.

Company culture is often underappreciated for the leadership leverage it can provide if well led. It allows midlevel managers and senior executives to extend their sway across hundreds of teams in ways not otherwise achievable. When well-conceived and widely accepted, a firm's culture can thus serve as a force multiplier for a manager's leadership, though only if periodically and properly updated. Then, said Gorsky, the credo's company-wide leadership value was sure to "outlive us" all.[59]

2. Build Architecture

In 2018, Alphabet reported profits of $31 billion. Apple racked up $59 billion. Impressive, certainly, among the best numbers ever reported. But only one organization could claim *the* trophy that year. By which I mean the sterling silver, Tiffany-designed, 22-inch-high Vince Lombardi Trophy, topped with a silver football matching the real thing. It goes to *the* football franchise that has triumphed in the National Football League's championship, the Super Bowl.[60]

Like every owner of the NFL's 32 teams, the Philadelphia Eagles' Jeffrey Lurie had long imagined the jubilation of the trophy being handed to him as the winning team's owner with tens of millions of fans tuned in. His team had reached the Super Bowl in 2004, but there it succumbed to the New England Patriots. In a rematch in

Super Bowl LII on February 4, 2018, however, Lurie finally savored the ultimate moment in American football.

The New England Patriots had been leading 33–32 with 9:22 to go. Favored by 4.5 points going in, the Patriots had already won the Super Bowl in 2017, 2015, 2005, 2004, and 2002. And in this latest contest, Patriots quarterback Tom Brady had been on a roll, ultimately passing for 505 yards, the most ever in this game of games. But the Eagles, with a backup quarterback on the field, would add 10 unanswered points in the game's final nine minutes. It was an upset that would inspire a city long starved for a football championship, along with fans nationwide who savored the improbable—an upstart that beat the odds.

The leadership of any organization, we appreciate from both practical experience and academic research, begins not only with the top executive—the owner in this case—but also the top team—here the owner, president, head coach, and head of football operations. A firm's top team, its "inner circle," is first defined by its job titles—the denizens of the C-suite—but its impact depends on the solidarity within it. A cohesive inner circle, with a shared vision, mutual respect, and complementary expertise, should comprise more than a throng of siloed executives. We know from studies of organizational performance that firms with more cross-boundary collaboration report better results—and in this instance, it became an axiom of the Eagles' owner as well.

The Eagles' principal, president, head coach, and head of football operations had come to work relatively independently during Lurie's early years as franchise owner, focusing on executing their own functions and consulting less with one another. But realizing that their responsibilities were more interdependent than they might have supposed, Lurie sought to transcend their job titles. They retained clear lines of authority, each attending to their own knitting, but now they also worked on sharing their wisdom.

Eagles president Don Smolenski and football operations head Howie Roseman, for instance, opted to watch all the Eagles' games together, whether at home or away—a lapsed practice they had begun more than 15 years prior and now resumed as top executives. One had to have the stadium ready for a game, the other had to have the players ready for the game, and their day-to-day responsibilities could not have been more different. But their objectives were the same, and from sideline banter about the action on the field, their shared understanding of what would make a difference both on and off the field became mutually reinforcing. They added frequent sit-downs together, talking both football and business, and so did the franchise owner and football operations manager who worked hand-in-hand on player drafts and trading deadlines.

Three-quarters of the inner circle's members had been on payroll for some time. Lurie himself had taken ownership in 1995, Roseman had come in 2000, and Smolenski went back that far as well. But Lurie reasoned that his football team would perform better on the field if his top leaders also behaved like a team, united by more than longevity. He enlarged the concept of a connected inner circle of top managers to a "team of teams" scheme in which functional groups work to achieve their own goals but also do so in a collaborative fashion to advance company objectives. In the US Army, for instance, lapel colors signal an officer's specialty: green for special forces, yellow for armor, blue for infantry, and so forth. Yet when an officer is promoted to the rank of general, they wear black, regardless of their function, signaling that they are now responsible for the whole organization, even as they perform specific functions within it.

In the case of the Eagles, players assigned to a given position also became building blocks, part of "the players' room," and their elected representatives in turn pulled together on a players council that worked with other blocks, including the coaching staff, top management, and staff specialists focused on sports science, stadium operations, and community relations. "NFL players are prideful guys; they want the ball," explained player Brent Celek, then the longest-tenured player on the Eagles. Yet despite that, he said, head coach Doug Pederson worked to get "everyone involved, there are plays for everyone. You know that you are a big part of the team. The game strategy he creates means there is a role for everyone."

The team-of-teams metaphor was felt off the field as well. Players who filled the same slot in the lineup regularly dined together or devoted time to the community together. "When we ask a player to visit a school or the children's hospital, there's an immediate sense of 'I get it,'" reported Julie Hirshey, director of community relations. "There's no blocking energy, and because a player wants to do it, the whole position group goes."

Completing the inner circle proved one of Jeffrey Lurie's most consequential leadership initiatives. With C-suite occupants and players more involved in common cause, the owner strengthened a kind of lateral bond that transcended their separate functions, bolstering the operations of each as well as the shared performance of all. "When people know that the leaders at the top trust each other, that trickles down into the whole organization," said Tina D'Orazio, the owner's chief of staff. "The football side and the business side can have tensions, but we see them talk it out and hash it out."

What emerges from a close look at this enterprise is the power of the club's architecture to make a leadership difference. Lurie had built a winning scheme even if it required 20 years before he could hoist a trophy from it.

Chapter 14

The Board Director Leader's Checklist

Though management drives an enterprise's strategy and leadership, an oversight body or governing board can also play a high-stakes role in both, and company directors are increasingly called to partner with executives for doing so. Fortunately, many non-executive directors come with extensive experience in running their own enterprises and are thus more than ready to contribute to a firm's strategy and leadership.

The challenge is for them to bring that expertise regularly and systematically into their boardrooms—and for this, a set of *governance checklists* can prove a useful resource, mission-critical checklists for methodically engaging directors in a company's strategy and leadership along with the executives.[61]

We begin with a governance checklist for all parties concerned with leadership and governance—whether directors, executives, chairs, owners, or investors—with questions they would be wise to raise annually or even more often when building, guiding, and appraising their firm's governance. Though focused on boards for the sake of illustration, the governance checklists can be seen as templates for leadership in advisory committees, product teams, work crews, marketing groups, or just about any squad or assembly. And the leadership roles of board chairs can be extended to group heads and team captains.[62]

The ability of a governing board to partner with top management also depends much upon the leadership skills of the board chair,

Board Director Leader's Checklist 1: Questions for Directors and Executives

✓ Do company executives *and* directors have a compelling strategy for creating value and increasing advantage?

✓ Are company executives and directors capable of thinking and acting strategically?

✓ Is the firm's organization capable of executing its strategy?

✓ Do all executives and directors add value to the company's strategy and leadership?

whether independent or fused with the chief executive. Either way, here is a two-part checklist based on studies of board leadership in China, India, the United States, and elsewhere for selecting a new chair for the board. It references a prospective chair's personal and professional qualities, and it is intended to guide the thinking of an outgoing chair, the chief executive, other directors, and the board's governance committee.

For considering and interviewing candidates to join a governing board, including as chair, below is a question checklist based on the suggestions by a prominent US attorney who has consulted with many boards.[63]

Governing boards, like company management, are ever evolving in their own internal priorities and external demands upon them, and here for illustration is a checklist for directors and executives of US firms to consider in the years ahead, appreciating that the priorities on such a list will be different from those of past years and are likely to differ for other regions. Whatever the specific year-by-year or country-by-country items on the list, the main point is to make the identified priorities and demands in a given year and region salient when recruiting new directors and setting board agendas for that setting.[64]

Board Director Leader's Checklist 2: Criteria for Selecting a New Board Chair

Personal Capabilities

✓ Extensive business leadership experience, including crisis leadership

✓ Respect and confidence of other directors

✓ Collaborative and restrained in style

✓ Personally bonded with other directors

✓ Comfortable in own skin and station in life

✓ Resilient, with a drive to confront and surmount setbacks

✓ Complete candor and expectation of the same in others

Professional Qualities

✓ An experienced mentor of leadership in others

✓ Shows mastery of the company's central idea, strategy, and operating issues, and applies seasoned and judicious judgment

✓ Downplays self-interest and serves as a trusted counselor and partner of the CEO

✓ Displays a passion for corporate governance, including both monitoring and leadership

✓ Brings the personal time and emotional energy to devote to board leadership

✓ Listens well and draws out ideas, learns what other directors have on their minds, crystalizes directors' diverse views, facilitates expression of underlying concerns, and focuses deliberations

✓ Displays effective influence, corporate diplomacy, and constructive guidance

✓ Embodies integrity and expects it in all directors and executives

Board Director Leader's Checklist 3: Questions for Interviewing Board Candidates

✓ There are times when executives, owners, or governance watchdogs may try to exert pressure on directors for a certain outcome. If so, how did you or will you react in the boardroom?

✓ Have you ever served on a board where some directors were not, in your opinion, doing what was in the best interests of the corporation as a whole? What did you do?

✓ Tell me about a time when you strongly disagreed with another director about your firm's strategy or company leadership, and how the issues were resolved.

✓ How would you handle a situation where there is pressure to achieve short-term quarterly results at the risk of jeopardizing the firm's long-term company performance?

Board Director Leader's Checklist 4: Contemporary Issues for Directors and Executives in the United States

✓ Board performance takes center stage. Many boards are giving ever more attention to strengthening their own performance and responding to shortcomings identified in their annual self-assessments.

✓ Board composition is scrutinized. Board composition is under pressure to meet new business challenges and stakeholder expectations. Today's directors are more focused than ever on ensuring their boards have the right expertise and experience to be effective.

✓ Board diversity and inclusion gets attention. Stakeholders are more interested in board diversity, equity, and inclusion, and boards are increasingly focused on recruiting directors with a range of backgrounds and experiences.

✓ More pressure on board priorities and practices. Director priorities and performance continue to face scrutiny from owners, regulators, and other stakeholders, causing board practices to remain in the public spotlight, including environmental and social issues.

✓ Directors are more concerned about public health risks. Directors are actively working with executives to guide the company through the COVID-19 crisis and rebound from it.

In collaboration with the top management team, governing boards are also becoming more directly involved in overseeing firm risk and resilience, and here is a governance checklist for directors concerned with both.[65]

Board Director Leader's Checklist 5: Risk and Resilience Issues for Directors

✓ Directors are taking a more deliberative role in overseeing risk, helping to guide executives in managing the firm's risk appetite, risk tolerance, and risk readiness.

✓ Directors carry special responsibility for identifying hazards that can become disruptive or even disastrous if not detected and mitigated—including those caused by management.

✓ Directors can work with executives to caution against intuitive thinking that can lead company executives to misestimate high-impact but low-probability risks, and to bring more deliberative thinking into both the boardroom and executive suite.

✓ Recruiting directors with prior risk-management experience as an executive or director of another company onto to a company's board can strengthen the firm's engaged and deliberative oversight of risk.

✓ Directors can usefully guide and appraise company risks in the development of new products and services, posing critical questions and challenging executive assumptions.

✓ Directors can play a special role in pressing executives to substantiate their forecasts, anticipated results, and identified risks without micromanaging them.

✓ Board chairs can more proactively involve directors in substantive dialogue by strengthening the norms of informed and active engagement in risk oversight.

✓ Company directors can also recruit and coach their top executives to think more deliberatively about company threats.

Because company owners and investors come with their own sets of distinctive concerns, here is a final governance checklist for their consideration.[66]

Board Director Leader's Checklist 6: Questions for Owners and Investors

✓ Has the board picked the right board chair and established a procedure to identify the next?

✓ Does the chair conduct effective executive sessions and make sure that the chief executive is receiving true feedback from the directors?

✓ Is the chair able to work well with top executives—but also ready to ensure that a faltering CEO is either mentored or removed?

✓ Has the chair arranged a way for directors to communicate directly with owners and investors?

✓ Does the board annually evaluate the performance of the chair?

✓ Has the chair arranged for the best prepared directors to serve as chairs of the key committees?

✓ Does the chair regularly consult off-line with the other directors?

✓ Is the chair focusing the directors on the company's strategic challenges and leadership capabilities?

✓ Are the directors actively leading the company on key decisions in partnership with the executives, not just monitoring them?

Applying the Checklist: Lenovo's Globalization

To illustrate how these checklists can be applied, we turn to the world's largest personal-computer company, China's Lenovo Group, as it globalized its operations. We witness directors playing a central role in defining company strategy, leadership, and their integration for the company's globalization.[67]

Founded in 1984, Lenovo emerged as China's largest computer maker, but "In our world," explained chief executive Yang Yuanqing, "a high growth rate is hard to sustain if you only try to maintain your position in the China market." In response, Lenovo acquired IBM's personal computer division, and in doing so, actively embraced the four questions in Checklist 1 to strengthen the strategic thinking and leadership of its directors and executives. On the first question, for instance—are all board members and senior executives adding value to the company's strategy?—the company revamped its board's membership and procedures to strengthen the directors' multinational contributions. On the second question—is the postacquisition governing board and top team prepared to think and act strategically in presiding over their firm?—Lenovo expanded its directors' attention to include a focus on the strategy and leadership of the company's multinational operation.

During the year before Lenovo acquired IBM's personal computer division, Lenovo's nonindependent directors outnumbered independent directors four to three. Its postacquisition board, by contrast, was divided among five executive directors, three private

equity directors, and three independent directors. Prior to the acquisition, all seven of the directors were Chinese or of Chinese origin.
After the acquisition, four of the eleven directors were Americans.
Before the acquisition, board meetings had always been conducted
in Chinese, but afterward English became the medium. Going into
the acquisition, the executive chairman and chief executive were both
Chinese; coming out of the acquisition, the executive chairman was
Chinese and the CEO American. Ma Xuezheng, the company's CFO
at the time of the acquisition, explained: "This is going to be very
much an international company operated in an international fashion." And that now carried into the boardroom. Lenovo non-
executive director Shan Weijian added, "We don't want people to
have a feeling of takeover [by a] Chinese company of the American
company. We want an integration process [that] doesn't involve
which part takes which."[68]

After the acquisition, Lenovo's directors pressed for bringing
new directors onto the board who would add deep experience to the
firm's strategic and corporate leadership. The selection standards
for new board members, reported Yang, now came to include both
executive experience and strategic vision. For one board seat, for
instance, the company vetted more than 20 candidates, narrowed
the list to four finalists, and finally invited John Barter, who had
served as AlliedSignal's chief financial officer and president of its
35,000-employee automotive division. He became the final choice
because of his proven experience in leading a large profit-and-loss
company division.

In the wake of the IBM PC acquisition, Lenovo moved its directors from a relatively limited role in monitoring management to more
active engagement in the company's strategy and leadership. "The
IBM PC acquisition is a watershed," reported Lenovo founder and
executive chair Liu Chuanzhi. "Before that point the board of directors did not play much [of a role]." The board had been primarily concerned with audit and compensation, but after the acquisition it
would come to play a far larger role.

The strengthening of the Lenovo board brought directors into direct guidance of the integration strategy for merging Lenovo's and IBM's distinct operating styles. IBM had built a business model around strong enduring relations with select corporate customers; Lenovo, by contrast, had created a more transactional model with many retail customers. Although large-enterprise relationships had been the staple of IBM's PC sales, Lenovo management anticipated greater global growth on the retail side, and it sought strategic guidance from the company's reconstituted board on optimal opportunities for building that model abroad.

To ensure a disciplined alignment of strategy and leadership, Lenovo formed a board-designated strategy committee, charged with vetting the company's mid- and long-term decisions on behalf of the directors. It included two Chinese executive directors—Yang Yuanqing and Liu Chuanzhi—and two American nonexecutive directors—James Coulter, a founding partner of the private equity firm Texas Pacific Group, and William Grabe, a managing director of private equity firm General Atlantic.

The Lenovo board met quarterly, but the strategy committee met monthly on issues ranging from company direction to cultural integration. The committee served as an "impartial third party," reported executive chair Yang, to help prevent a "confrontation" between the Chinese- and American-heritage divisions of the company. In the experience of CEO William Amelio, the directors worked with him and the other executives to pick from an array of choices to identify "the right idea that is going to maximize the core competence of the company."

The Lenovo directors also became directly engaged in decisions on executive succession—the key choices on the company's leadership, an arena that had not been the board's prerogative before the IBM PC acquisition. Coulter and Grabe, the two independent directors from the private equity groups, played a pivotal role in the early replacement of the first CEO after the IBM acquisition. At the time of the transaction, IBM's Stephen Ward had seemed the logical

candidate for the role of chief executive, with Yang to serve as executive chairman, but within several months it was evident to the
board's strategy committee that Ward's leadership was not a good
fit with the firm's new direction. Supply chain efficiencies were
going to be critical to ensure the profitability of the combined companies, but the first CEO did not come with the requisite experience
for optimizing those efficiencies in an extremely cost-conscious
market.

In applying the second question in Board Director Leader's
Checklist 1—that of whether top executives are capable of thinking
and acting strategically—the board pressed for Lenovo's officers to
reflect the company's new operating geographies. Of the top management team in 2004, a year before the acquisition, all were Chinese;
of the 18 members of the top management team in 2007, two years
after the purchase, six were from greater China, one from Europe,
and 11 from the United States.

In line with part of the fourth question in Board Director Leader's
Checklist 1—do all directors add value to Lenovo's strategy and
leadership?—Lenovo made a point to bring a host of strategic issues
to the board for its vetting and final decision-making. The issues
included how long to retain the IBM logo on its products (the acquisition agreement had allowed for five years), what new acquisitions
to pursue, which adjacent product areas to enter, and whether to build
devices that bridge laptops and desktops.

The strategy committee in particular went "through all the
options and thoroughly [vetted] the pros and cons of the various
courses of action," said the CEO Amelio. The two American directors from the private equity firms brought extensive experience in
acquisitions that made them particularly valuable for appraising prospective decisions, in the experience of Amelio. They were "totally
invaluable," he said, "because the name of their game is lots of acquisitions and mergers."

When Lenovo executives considered acquiring another personal
computer maker, the strategy committee and even the full board
became actively engaged on whether to proceed and, if so, what to

pay. "Everybody was involved," reported nonexecutive Shan Weijian, "because this is a large issue for the entire company." Lenovo decided to back off, guided by the board's skepticism about the deal's potential value.

The board's strategy committee also played a particularly important role in appraising the company's leadership. The executive chair and chief executive submitted annual self-assessments and 360-degree feedback results to the committee and the board, and the directors then evaluated the extent to which the executives had achieved their annual plan's financial, market-share, talent recruitment, and related goals.

In line with the several governance leadership checklists proposed here, we saw a sharp divide between the way the Lenovo board operated before and after its decision to build out globally with the IBM PC division acquisition. Prior to the purchase, the board had operated without a strategy committee or an annual performance review. Now it had both. Director decisions before had been largely limited to accounting audit and shareholder rights. Now their decisions ranged from branding to sourcing, and more generally from strategy to leadership.

Directors thus played a far larger role in company strategy and leadership in the wake of the IBM acquisition. They had replaced the first chief executive, decided against an acquisition, and facilitated cross-cultural integration of widely different divisions. A decade after the IBM PC acquisition and remake of its board and management to better strategize and lead the company, Lenovo had the largest global market share of PC sales.

To draw the best from a governing board, developing a set of governance leadership checklists is a way to help ensure both directors and executives are attentive in detail to the mission-critical features of what makes for an optimal combination of strategy and leadership in your boardrooms.

Conclusion
The Owner's Manual

The Leader's Checklist is meant to serve as a trigger to leadership action. To work well, it should be rooted in practical experience and analytic evidence; include all the mission-critical principles for effective application; be adapted and customized to your place and times; and be extended to your teams, your teams of teams, and your enterprises as a whole and their governing bodies.

Above all, the several checklists should be actively and recurrently used to guide your decisions and define your actions. It is wise to avoid convening online assemblies, off-sites, creative brainstorming, or board meetings without them. In doing so, you can use each of the checklist principles to generate a set of questions that will help you test, retest, refine, and update your preparedness for almost any situation. Here are prompts for each of the 16 primary precepts:

1. **Articulate a Vision.**
   - Do my direct reports see the forest, not just the trees?
   - Does everyone in the firm know not only where we are going, but why?
   - Is the destination compelling and appealing?
2. **Think and Act Strategically.**
   - Do we have a realistic plan both for creating short-term results and for mapping out the future?
   - Have we considered all the players and anticipated every roadblock?

- Has everybody embraced—and can everybody explain—the firm's competitive strategy and value drivers?

3. **Honor the Room.**
   - Do those in the room know that you respect and value their talents and efforts?
   - Have you made it clear that their upward guidance is always sought?
   - Is there a sense of engagement on the front lines, and do they see themselves as "us," not "them"?

4. **Take Charge and Lead Change.**
   - Are you prepared to take charge even when you are not fully or formally in charge?
   - If so, do you come with the capacity and position to embrace responsibility?
   - For the technical decisions ahead, are you ready to delegate but not abdicate?

5. **Act Decisively.**
   - Are most of your decisions both good and timely?
   - Do you convey your strategic intent and then let others reach their own decisions?
   - Is your own decision threshold close to a "70%" go point?

6. **Communicate Persuasively.**
   - Are the messages about vision, strategy, and execution crystal clear and indelible?
   - Have you mobilized all communication channels, from purely personal to social media?
   - Can you deliver a compelling account before the elevator passes the 10th floor?

7. **Motivate the Workforce.**
   - Have you identified each person's "hot button" and focused on it?
   - Do you work personal pride and shared purpose into most communications?
   - Are you keeping your powder dry for those urgent moments when you may need it?

8. **Embrace the Front Lines.**
   - Have you made your intent clear and empowered those around you to act?
   - Do you regularly meet with those in direct contact with customers?
   - Is everybody able to communicate their ideas and concerns to you?

9. **Build Leadership in Others.**
   - Are all managers expected to build leadership among their subordinates?
   - Does the company culture foster the effective exercise of leadership?
   - Are leadership development opportunities available to most, if not all, managers?

10. **Manage Relations.**
    - Is the hierarchy reduced to a minimum, and does bad news travel up?
    - Are managers self-aware and empathetic?
    - Are autocratic, egocentric, and irritable behaviors censured?

11. **Identify Personal Implications.**
    - Do employees appreciate how the firm's vision and strategy impact them individually?
    - What private sacrifices will be necessary for achieving the common cause?
    - How will the plan affect people's personal livelihood and quality of work life?

12. **Convey Your Character.**
    - Have you communicated your commitment to performance with integrity?
    - Do those in the organization know you as a person, and do they appreciate your aspirations and your agendas?
    - Have you been in the same room or at least on the same call with everybody who works with you during the past year?

13. **Dampen Overoptimism and Excessive Pessimism.**
    - Have you prepared the organization for unlikely but extremely consequential events?
    - Do you celebrate success but also guard against the by-products of excessive confidence?
    - Have you paved the way not only for quarterly results but for long-term performance?
14. **Build a Diverse Top Team.**
    - Have you drawn quality performers into your inner circle?
    - Are they diverse in expertise but united in purpose?
    - Are they as engaged, energized, and included as you?
15. **Place Common Interest First.**
    - Have you contributed to or even helped define the enterprise's purpose?
    - In all decisions, have you placed shared resolve ahead of private gain?
    - Do the firm's vision and strategy embody the organization's mission?
16. **Think Like a Chief Executive.**
    - Are you reasoning like a president or CEO even if you are unlikely to become one?
    - If you were the company CEO, what would she or he expect of your leadership now?
    - Have you pulled all your functions and operations under a common umbrella?

Not all the questions are necessarily applicable to every situation, but it is the universal questioning that counts—as a goad to implementation, or whether you are facing a typical day at the office, keynoting an off-site event, firing up an online gathering, or confronting an emergent crisis. And it is the 16 principles behind the questions that when taken together constitute a minimalist but mission-critical leader's checklist; each precept is to be embraced when leadership really matters, especially during periods of uncertainty and change when one's leadership actions—or inactions—become most fateful.

And the same for the team leader's checklist, the team of teams checklist, and governance leadership checklists. When close at hand, they should all help us avoid unforced errors and, more importantly, embrace the leadership we require for reaching a more promising land.

Notes

1   Michael Useem, *The Edge: How 10 CEOs Learned to Lead—and the Lessons for Us All* (New York: PublicAffairs, 2021).

2   Among the organizations are Abbott Laboratories, Accenture, ADP, American Express, Amgen, Berkshire Partners, Canadian Imperial Bank of Commerce, Cargill, CEO Academy, Citigroup, Cisco Systems, CITIC Bank (China), Coca-Cola, Columbia Energy, Comcast, Computer Sciences Corporation, Daimler, Deloitte, DuPont, Entergy, Eli Lilly, Estée Lauder Companies, Federal Executive Institute, Fidelity Investments, GlaxoSmithKline, Goldman Sachs, Google, Grupo Santander (Chile), Hartford Insurance, Hearst, Hewlett-Packard, HSM, IBM, ICICI Bank (India), Intel, Johnson & Johnson, Kimberly-Clark, KPMG, Liberty Mutual Insurance, Lucent Technologies, MassMutual, Mastercard, McGraw-Hill, Medtronic, Merck, Microsoft, Milliken, Morgan Stanley, Motorola, the National Football League, the New York City Fire Department, the New York Times Company, Nokia, Northrop Grumman, Novartis, Penske, Petrobras (Brazil), Pew Charitable Trusts, PricewaterhouseCoopers, Progressive Insurance, Raytheon, Samsung, Securities Association of China, Siemens, Singapore General Hospital, Sprint, 3Com Corporation, Thomson Financial, Toyota, Travelers, Verizon, United Healthcare, United Technologies, the UN Development Programme, the US Department of Justice, the US Department of Veterans Affairs, the US Marine Corps, the US Military Academy, and the World Economic Forum. I have also annually worked on leadership development with 100 to 220 students enrolled in the Wharton Executive MBA program.

3   Albert Einstein, "On the Method of Theoretical Physics," *Philosophy of Science* 1 (1934): 163–69.

4   "IBM to Acquire Red Hat," Red Hat, October 28, 2018, https://www.redhat.com /en/about/press-releases/ibm-acquire-red-hat-completely-changing-cloud -landscape-and-becoming-worlds-1-hybrid-cloud-provider.

5   Statista, Global Quarterly Market Share of Cloud Infrastructure Services from 2017 to 2020, by Vendor, https://www.statista.com/statistics/477277/cloud -infrastructure-services-market-share.

6   Howard Gardner with Emma Laskin, *Leading Minds: An Anatomy of Leadership* (New York: Basic Books, 1996).

7   David F. Freedman, *Corps Business: The 30 Management Principles of the U.S. Marines* (New York: Harper Business, 1996); Michael Useem, "Four Lessons in

Adaptive Leadership," *Harvard Business Review*, November 2010; "Lead Time," an interview with Warren Bennis, *World Link* magazine, January–February 1999.

8   Adam Bryant, "Never Duck the Tough Questions," *New York Times*, July 17, 2011; Adam Bryant, "Imagining a World of No Annual Reviews," *New York Times*, October 17, 2011. For leaders describing the capacities that have made the greatest difference to them, see Adam Bryant, *The Corner Office: Indispensable and Unexpected Lessons from CEOs on How to Lead and Succeed* (New York: Times Books, 2011); Mukul Pandya, Robbie Shell, and Nightly Business Report, *Lasting Leadership: What You Can Learn from the Top 25 Business People of Our Times* (Philadelphia: Wharton School Publishing and Boston: Pearson Education, 2004); Louis V. Gerstner Jr., *Who Says Elephants Can't Dance? How I Turned Around IBM* (New York: HarperCollins, 2003); Bill George, *Authentic Leadership: Rediscovering the Secrets to Creating Lasting Value* (Hoboken, NJ: Jossey-Bass, 2004); see also the *New York Times* "Corner Office" web page, at http://projects.nytimes.com/corner-office, the *Wall Street Journal*'s "Lessons in Leadership" web page, at http://online.wsj.com/public/page/lessons-in -leadership.html?mod=WSJ_topnav_na_business, and the *Washington Post*'s "On Leadership" web page, at http://www.washingtonpost.com/national/on -leadership.

9   Peter Drucker, "Not Enough Generals Were Killed," in *The Leader of the Future*, edited by Frances Hesselbein, Marshall Goldsmith, and Richard Beckhard (Hoboken, NJ: Jossey-Bass, 1996); Noel Tichy, *The Leadership Engine: How Winning Companies Build Leaders at Every Level* (New York: HarperCollins, 1997); Geoffrey Colvin, "How to Build Great Leaders," *Fortune*, November 20, 2009; Hewitt Associates, *Top Companies for Leaders* (Hewitt Associates, 2009).

10 Frances Hesselbein, *My Life in Leadership: The Journey and Lessons Learned Along the Way* (Hoboken, NJ: Jossey-Bass, 2011); Daniel Goleman, "What Makes a Leader?" *Harvard Business Review*, November–December 1998, 93–102; Robert J. House, Paul J. Hanges, Mansour Javidan, Peter W. Dorfman, and Vipin Gupta, eds., *Culture, Leadership, and Organizations: The GLOBE Study of 62 Societies* (Thousand Oaks, CA: Sage Publications, 2004); Mansour Javidan, Peter W. Dorfman, Mary Sully de Luque, and Robert J. House, "In the Eye of the Beholder: Cross Cultural Lessons in Leadership from Project GLOBE," *Academy of Management Perspectives* 20 (2006): 67–90. For examples of other academic assessments, see Nitin Nohria and Rakesh Khurana, eds., *Handbook of Leadership Theory and Practice* (Cambridge, MA: Harvard Business Press, 2010), and articles appearing in the *Leadership Quarterly*.

11 Jay W. Lorsch and Thomas J. Tierney, *Aligning the Stars: How to Succeed When Professionals Drive Results* (Cambridge, MA: Harvard Business Press, 2002).

12 Michael Useem, *Investor Capitalism: How Money Managers Are Changing the Face of Corporate America* (New York: Basic Books/HarperCollins, 1996); Michael Useem, "How Well-Run Boards Make Decisions," *Harvard Business Review*, November 2006, 130–38; Michael Useem and Andy Zelleke, "Oversight

and Delegation in Corporate Governance: Deciding What the Board Should Decide," *Corporate Governance: An International Review* 14 (2006): 2–12; Michael Useem, "The Ascent of Shareholder Monitoring and Strategic Partnering: The Dual Functions of the Corporate Board," in *Sage Handbook on Corporate Governance*, edited by Thomas Clarke and Doug Branson (Thousand Oaks, CA: Sage Publications, 2012).

13 House, Hanges, Javidan, Dorfman, and Gupta, *Culture, Leadership, and Organizations*; Javidan et al., "In the Eye of the Beholder: Cross Cultural Lessons in Leadership from Project GLOBE," *Academy of Management Perspectives* 20 (2006): 67–90.

14 Peter Cappelli, Harbir Singh, Jitendra Singh, and Michael Useem, *The India Way: How India's Top Business Leaders Are Revolutionizing Management* (Cambridge, MA: Harvard Business Press, 2010).

15 Michael Useem, Harbir Singh, Neng Liang, and Peter Cappelli, *Fortune Makers: The Leaders Creating China's Great Global Companies* (New York: PublicAffairs, 2017); Michael Useem, "Leading Large Companies in the U.S. and Other National Settings: What Will Be the Same, and What May Be Different?," in *The Study and Practice of Global Leadership*, edited by Gama Perruci (International Leadership Association Building Leadership Bridges Series, Emerald Group Publishing, 2022 [forthcoming]).

16 John P. Kotter and Dan S. Cohen, *The Heart of Change: Real-Life Stories of How People Change Their Organizations* (Cambridge, MA: Harvard Business Press, 2002); see also David A. Nadler and Michael L. Tushman, "Beyond the Charismatic Leader: Leadership and Organizational Change," *California Management Review* 32 (Winter 1990): 77–97; Charles A. O'Reilly III and Michael L. Tushman, *Winning Through Innovation: A Practical Guide to Leading Organizational Change and Renewal* (Cambridge, MA: Harvard Business Press, 2002).

17 Dennis Carey, Michael Patsalos-Fox, and Michael Useem, "Leadership Lessons for Hard Times," *McKinsey Quarterly*, July 2009.

18 This paragraph is drawn from Useem, *The Edge*. See, for instance, "Measuring the Community Connection: A Strategy Checklist for Leaders," American Hospital Association, 2006, http://www.caringforcommunities.org /caringforcommunities/content/strategychecklist.pdf; William G. Bowen, *Lessons Learned: Reflections of a University President* (Princeton, NJ: Princeton University Press, 2010); Jim Collins, *Good to Great and the Social Sectors* (New York: HarperCollins, 2005); Marshall Ganz, *Why David Sometimes Wins: Leadership, Organization, and Strategy in the California Farm Worker Movement* (New York: Oxford University Press, 2010); John W. Gardner, *On Leadership* (New York: Free Press, 1993); General Accounting Office, *Human Capital: A Self-Assessment Checklist for Agency Leaders* (Washington, DC: GAO, 1999); David Gergen, *Eyewitness to Power: The Essence of Leadership from Nixon to Clinton* (New York: Simon & Schuster, 2001); Mel Gill, Robert J. Flynn, and Elke

Reissing, "The Governance Self-Assessment Checklist: An Instrument for
Assessing Board Effectiveness," *Nonprofit Management and Leadership* 15
(2005): 271–94; Doris Kearns Goodwin, *Team of Rivals: The Political Genius of
Abraham Lincoln* (New York: Simon & Schuster, 2005); Nannerl O. Keohane,
Higher Ground: Ethics and Leadership in the Modern University (Durham, NC:
Duke University Press, 2006); Mike Krzyzewski and Donald T. Phillips, *Leading
with the Heart: Coach K's Successful Strategies for Basketball, Business, and Life*
(New York: Business Plus/Hachette, 2001); Pat Summit, *Reach for the Summit* (New
York: Broadway Books, 1999); D. Michael Lindsay, *Faith in the Halls of Power:
How Evangelicals Joined the American Elite* (New York: Oxford University
Press, 2008); Joe Torre and Henry Dreher, *Joe Torre's Ground Rules for Winners:
12 Keys to Managing Team Players, Tough Bosses, Setbacks, and Success* (New
York: Hyperion, 2000); Barbara Turnbull, "Evaluating School-Based
Management: A Tool for Team Self-Review," *International Journal of
Leadership in Education* 8 (2005): 73–79; John Wooden and Steve Jamison,
Wooden on Leadership: How to Create a Winning Organization (New York:
McGraw-Hill, 2005); and "Filling in the 'Missing Pieces': How Mary Ellen
Iskenderian and Women's World Banking Are Redefining Microfinance,"
Knowledge@Wharton, July 7, 2010, http://knowledge.wharton.upenn.edu/article
.cfm?articleid=2540.

19 Samuel Linn, Alpha Company, 52nd Infantry Regiment (AT), 5/2 Stryker
Brigade Combat Team, U.S. Army, Kandahar, Afghanistan, 2009–2010, personal
communication; Center for Army Lessons Learned, http://usacac.army.mil/cac2
/call/index.asp (not available to the public).

20 National Interagency Fire Center, *Incident Response Pocket Guide*, January 2010,
http://www.nwcg.gov/pms/pubs/pubs.htm (also available as an iPad app, iRPG);
New York City Fire Department, Chief Officer Operational Checklists,
November 16, 2005.

21 Pre-Sales Checklist prepared by Ralf Klein and John Gobron, Microsoft,
personal communication, 2010.

22 John Baldoni, *Lead Your Boss: The Subtle Art of Managing Up* (New York:
Amacom, 2009); John J. Gabarro and John P. Kotter, "Managing Your Boss,"
Harvard Business Review, January 2005; Michael Useem, *Leading Up: How to Lead
Your Boss So You Both Win* (New York: Crown Business/Random House, 2002).

23 Bryant, "Google's Quest to Build a Better Boss," *New York Times*, March 12, 2011.

24 Michael Useem, Michael Barriere, and Joseph Ryan, "Looking South to See
North: Upward Appraisal of Tangible Leadership," Wharton Center for
Leadership and Change, University of Pennsylvania, 2011.

25 Atul Gawande, *The Checklist Manifesto: How to Get Things Right* (New York:
Holt, 2009); Alex B. Haynes et al., "A Surgical Safety Checklist to Reduce
Morbidity and Mortality in a Global Population," *New England Journal of
Medicine* 360 (2009): 491–99; John D. Brinkmeyer, "Strategies for Improving
Surgical Quality—Checklists and Beyond," *New England Journal of Medicine*

363 (2010): 1963–65; Eefje N. de Vries et al., "Effect of a Comprehensive Surgical Safety System on Patient Outcomes," *New England Journal of Medicine* 363 (2010): 1928–37.

26 Jeffrey Pfeffer and Robert I. Sutton, *The Knowing-Doing Gap: How Smart Companies Turn Knowledge into Action* (Cambridge, MA: Harvard Business School Press, 2000).

27 Michael Useem, *The Leadership Moment: Nine True Stories of Triumph and Disaster and Their Lessons for Us All* (New York: Times Books/Random House, 1998).

28 Norman Maclean, *Young Men and Fire* (Chicago: University of Chicago Press, 1993); Useem, *The Leadership Moment*; Michael Useem; "In the Heat of the Moment: A Case Study in Life-and-Death Decision Making," *Fortune*, June 27, 2005.

29 The account that follows draws on Useem, *The Leadership Moment* (and a number of sources cited therein), and Roy Vagelos and Louis Galambos, *Medicine, Science, and Merck* (Cambridge: Cambridge University Press, 2004).

30 William C. Campbell, Nobel Prize in Physiology or Medicine, 2015, https://www .nobelprize.org/prizes/medicine/2015/campbell/facts.

31 This section draws upon Dennis Carey, Brian Dumaine, Michael Useem, and Rodney Zemmel, *Go Long: Why Long-Term Thinking Is Your Best Short-Term Strategy* (Philadelphia: Wharton School Press, 2018).

32 John Chambers, *Connecting the Dots: Lessons for Leadership in a Startup World* (New York: Hachette Books, 2018); Eric Schmidt, Jonathan Rosenberg, and Alan Eagle, *Trillion Dollar Coach: The Leadership Playbook of Silicon Valley's Bill Campbell* (New York: Harper Business, 2019).

33 Michael Useem, "John Chambers: Whether Up or Down, Always Innovating," *U.S. News & World Report*, November 2009; the phrase "touching the void" is borrowed from Joe Simpson, *Touching the Void: The True Story of One Man's Miraculous Survival* (New York: Perennial, 2004).

34 D. A. Waldman, G. G. Ramirez, R. J. House, and P. Puranan, "Does Leadership Matter? CEO Leadership Attributes and Profitability Under Conditions of Perceived Environmental Uncertainty," *Academy of Management Journal* 44 (2001), 134–43; Alan Berkeley Thomas, "Does Leadership Make a Difference to Organizational Performance?" *Administrative Science Quarterly* 33 (1988): 388–400; Stanley Lieberson and James F. O'Connor, "Leadership and Organizational Performance: A Study of Large Corporations," *American Sociological Review* 37 (1972): 117–30.

35 We draw upon several sources, including American International Group, Inc., *2008 Annual Report*; Roddy Boyd, *Fatal Risk: A Cautionary Tale of AIG's Corporate Suicide* (Hoboken, NJ: Wiley, 2011); Eric Dickinson, "Credit Default Swaps: So Dear to Us, So Dangerous," Social Science Research Network, November 20, 2008, https://papers.ssrn.com/sol3/papers.cfm?abstract_id

=1315535; Eric Dinallo, Testimony to the U.S. Senate Committee on Banking, Housing, and Urban Affairs, March 5, 2009; Donald L. Kohn, Statement to the U.S. Senate Committee on Banking, Housing, and Urban Affairs, March 5, 2009; Ben Levisohn, "AIG's CDS Hoard: The Great Unraveling," *Business Week Online,* April 7, 2009; Steve Lohr, "In Modeling Risk, the Human Factor Was Left Out," *New York Times,* November 5, 2008; Nell Minow, Testimony to the U.S. House of Representatives Committee on Oversight and Government Reform, October 7, 2008; Carrick Mollenkamp, Serena Ng, Liam Pleven, and Randall Smith, "Behind AIG's Fall, Risk Models Failed to Pass Real-World Test," *Wall Street Journal,* October 31, 2008; Gretchen Morgenson, "Behind Insurer's Crisis, Blind Eye to a Web of Risk," *New York Times,* September 28, 2008; Scott M. Polakoff, Statement to the U.S. Senate Committee on Banking, Housing, and Urban Affairs, March 5, 2009; William K. Sjostrom Jr., "The AIG Bailout," *Washington and Lee Law Review* 66 (2009): 943–991; and Gillian Tett, *Fool's Gold: How Unrestrained Greed Corrupted a Dream, Shattered Markets, and Unleashed a Catastrophe* (New York: Little, Brown, 2009).

36 Morgenson, "Behind Insurer's Crisis, Blind Eye to a Web of Risk."

37 Levisohn, "AIG's CDS Hoard: The Great Unraveling."

38 Morgenson, "Behind Insurer's Crisis, Blind Eye to a Web of Risk"; Minow, Testimony to the U.S. House of Representatives Committee on Oversight and Government Reform, 2008.

39 Polakoff, Statement to the U.S. Senate Committee on Banking, Housing, and Urban Affairs, 2009.

40 Itzhak Ben-David, John R. Graham, and Campbell R. Harvey, "Managerial Overconfidence and Corporate Policies," Social Science Research Network, 2021, https://papers.ssrn.com/sol3/papers.cfm?abstract_id=1079308; Anand M. Goel and Anjan V. Thakor, "Overconfidence, CEO Selection, and Corporate Governance," *Journal of Finance* 63 (2008): 2737–84; Haim Mano, "Risk-Taking, Framing Effects, and Affect," *Organizational Behavior and Human Decision Processes* 57 (1994): 38–58; William F. Wright, "Mood Effects on Subjective Probability Assessment," *Organizational Behavior and Human Decision Processes* 52 (1992): 276–91.

41 Useem, *The Leadership Moment;* for useful illustrations of learning leadership from leaders' failures, not just exemplary behavior, see *Harvard Business Review,* "The Failure Issue: How to Understand It, Learn from It, and Recover from It," April 2011; Sydney Finkelstein, *Why Smart Executives Fail and What You Can Learn from Their Mistakes,* (New York: Portfolio, 2003); Tim Irwin, *Derailed: Five Lessons Learned from Catastrophic Failures of Leadership* (New York: Thomas Nelson, 2009); Robert E. Mittelstaedt Jr., *Will Your Next Mistake Be Fatal? Avoiding the Chain of Mistakes That Can Destroy Your Organization* (New York: Pearson, 2004); Jeffrey Sonnenfeld and Andrew Ward, *Firing Back: How Great Leaders Rebound from Career Decisions* (Cambridge, MA: Harvard Business Press, 2007).

42   Jonathan Franklin, *33 Men: Inside the Miraculous Survival and Dramatic Rescue of the Chilean Miners* (New York: Putnam, 2011); Rodrigo Jordán, Matko Koljatic, and Michael Useem, "Leading the Rescue of the Miners in Chile," Wharton School, Business Case, 2011; Michael Useem, Rodrigo Jordán, and Matko Koljatic, "33 Below: Learning Crisis Leadership and General Management from the Rescue of the Miners in Chile," Wharton Center for Leadership, University of Pennsylvania, 2011. Adapted from the *Knowledge@Wharton* interview first published June 22, 2011. For a link to the video interview, visit http://wdp.wharton.upenn.edu/books/the-leaders-checklist.

43   The narrative and direct quotes are from sources cited in the prior endnote. In preparing those articles, we drew upon the extensive media coverage of the rescue and personal interviews with the leader of the rescue and the members of the rescue team: René Aguilar, head of safety, El Teniente mine, Codelco (National Copper Corporation of Chile), and deputy chief on rescue site, December 22, 2010; Cristián Barra, cabinet chief, Ministry of the Interior, Republic of Chile, January 5, 2010; Laurence Golborne, mining minister, Republic of Chile, November 1, 2010; Luz Granier, chief of staff to the mining minister, November 1, 2010; and André Sougarret, manager, El Teniente mine, Codelco, and chief engineer on rescue site, January 5, 2010.

44   For a case on the rescue by Rodrigo Jordán, Matko Koljatic, and Michael Useem, "Leading the Rescue of the Miners in Chile," Wharton School, Business Case, 2011 (http://kw.wharton.upenn.edu/wdp/files/2011/07/Leading-the-Miners -Rescue.pdf). A special exhibit on the rescue, *Against All Odds: Rescue at the Chilean Mine*, was opened by the Smithsonian Institution and the Embassy of Chile at the National Museum of Natural History in Washington, DC, in August 2011 (http://www.si.edu/exhibitions/ details/Against-All-Odds-Rescue-at-the-Chilean-Mine-4694). For an article that more fully examines the leadership of Laurence Golborne, see Michael Useem, Rodrigo Jordán, and Matko Koljatic, "33 Below: Learning Crisis Leadership from the Rescue of the Miners in Chile," *MIT Sloan Management Review* (Fall 2011), http://sloanreview .mit.edu/the-magazine/2011-fall/53106/how-to-lead-during-a-crisis-lessons-from -the-rescue-of-the-chilean-miners; "Rescue of the 33 Miners: An Interview with Chile's Mining Minister Laurence Golborne," interview with Michael Useem, *Knowledge@Wharton*, June 22, 2011, http://wdp.wharton.upenn.edu/books/the -leaders-checklist.

45   Helene Cooper, "Medal of Honor for Bravery in Afghanistan," *New York Times*, November 16, 2011; also see http://www.army.mil/medalofhonor/giunta/citation .html and http://www.youtube.com/watch?v=R2RWscJM97U.

46   British Petroleum, *Deepwater Horizon: Accident Investigation Report*, September 8, 2010; National Commission on the BP Deepwater Horizon Oil Spill and Offshore Drilling, *Deep Water: The Gulf Oil Disaster and the Future of Offshore Drilling*, January 11, 2011; Michael Lewis, *The Big Short: Inside the Doomsday Machine* (New York: Norton, 2011); Andrew Ross Sorkin, *Too Big to Fail: The Inside Story of How Wall Street and Washington Fought to Save the*

Financial System—and Themselves (New York: Viking Press, 2009); Bethany McLean and Joe Nocera, *All the Devils Are Here: The Hidden History of the Financial Crisis* (New York: Portfolio, 2010).

47   Peter Elkind and Jennifer Reingold with Doris Burke, "Inside Pfizer's Palace Coup," *Fortune*, August 15, 2011.

48   Gerald F. Davis, *Managed by the Markets: How Finance Re-Shaped America* (Oxford: Oxford University Press, 2009); Bill McNabb, Ram Charan, and Dennis Carey, *Talent, Strategy and Risk* (Cambridge, MA: Harvard Business Review Press, 2021); Michael Useem, *Investor Capitalism: How Money Managers Are Changing the Face of Corporate America* (New York: Basic Books/HarperCollins, 1996); Michael Useem, "Corporate Leadership in a Globalizing Equity Market," *Academy of Management Executive* 12 (1998): 43–59.

49   Michael Useem, "The Business of Employment: Time to Revise Investor Capitalism's Mantra," On Leadership, *Washington Post*, August 9, 2011, http://www.washingtonpost.com/national/onleadership/the-business-of -employment-time-to-revise-investorcapitalisms-mantra/2011/08/09 /gIQAh8rs4I_story.html.

50   *9/11: The Filmmakers' Commemorative Edition*, directed by Gedeon Naudet, James Hanlon, and Jules Naudet, Paramount (2002).

51   Adam Goodheart, *1861: The Civil War Awakening* (New York: Knopf, 2011); Drew Gilpin Faust, *This Republic of Suffering: Death and the American Civil War* (New York: Knopf, 2008).

52   Joshua Lawrence Chamberlain, *Passing of the Armies: The Last Campaign of the Armies* (Gettysburg, PA: Stan Clark Military Books, 1994), 261.

53   Chamberlain, *Passing of the Armies*; Douglas Southall Freeman, *Lee's Lieutenants: A Study in Command*, abridged in one volume by Stephen W. Sears (New York: Scribners, 1998); William Marvel, *Lee's Last Retreat: The Flight to Appomattox* (Durham, NC: University of North Carolina Press, 2002); Alice Rains Trulock, *In the Hands of Providence: Joshua L. Chamberlain and the American Civil War* (Durham, NC: University of North Carolina Press, 1992); Jay Winik, *April 1865: The Month That Saved America* (New York: HarperCollins, 2001).

54   This section draws on Useem, *The Edge*.

55   Martine Haas and Mark Mortensen, "The Secrets of Great Teamwork," *Harvard Business Review*, June 2016.

56   Michael Useem, "Making Better Choices," *Financial Times*, March 31, 2006.

57   Stanley McChrystal with Tantum Collins, David Silverman, and Chris Fussell, *Team of Teams: New Rules of Engagement for a Complex World* (New York: Portfolio/Penguin, 2015).

58   This section draws on Useem, *The Edge*.

59   Useem, *The Edge*.

60 This section draws on Useem, *The Edge*.

61 Ram Charan, Dennis Carey, and Michael Useem, *Boards That Lead* (Cambridge, MA: Harvard Business Press, 2014).

62 Harbir Singh and Michael Useem, *The Strategic Leader's Roadmap* (Philadelphia: Wharton School Press, 2021).

63 Ira M. Millstein, *The Activist Director* (New York: Columbia Business School Publishing, 2016).

64 Cappelli, H. Singh, J. Singh, and Useem, *The India Way*; PricewaterhouseCoopers, *PwC's 2020 Annual Corporate Directors Survey*, https://www.pwc.com/us/en/services/governance-insights-center/library/annual-corporate-directors-survey.html.

65 Howard Kunreuther and Michael Useem, *Mastering Catastrophic Risk* (New York: Oxford University Press, 2020).

66 Michael Useem, *Investor Capitalism* (New York: Basic Books, 1996).

67 Useem, Singh, Liang, and Cappelli, *Fortune Makers*.

68 Michael Useem and Neng Liang, "Globalizing the Company Board: Lessons from China's Lenovo," in *Leading Corporate Boardrooms: The New Realities, the New Rules*, edited by Jay Conger (San Francisco: Jossey-Bass, 2009).

Index

Page numbers in italics refer to figures.

About the Author

Michael Useem is Professor of Management and Faculty Director of the Center for Leadership and Change Management and McNulty Leadership Program at the Wharton School of the University of Pennsylvania. His university teaching includes MBA and executive MBA courses on management and leadership, and he offers programs on leadership and governance for managers in the United States, Asia, Europe, and Latin America. He works on leadership development with many companies and organizations in the private, public, and nonprofit sectors.

He is coanchor for the weekly program "Leadership in Action" on SiriusXM Radio Channel 132 and codirector of the annual CEO Academy. He is the author of *The Leader's Checklist*, *The Strategic Leader's Roadmap* (with Harbir Singh), *The Edge: How Ten CEOs Learned to Lead—And the Lessons for Us All*, *Go Long: Why Long-Term Thinking Is Your Best Short-Term Strategy* (with Dennis Carey, Brian Dumaine, and Rodney Zemmel), *Mastering Catastrophic Risk* (with Howard Kunreuther), *Fortune Makers: The Leaders Creating China's Great Global Companies* (with Harbir Singh, Neng Liang, and Peter Cappelli), *The India Way* (with Peter Cappelli, Harbir Singh, and Jitendra Singh), and *Boards That Lead* (with Ram Charan and Dennis Carey).

WHARTON
SCHOOL
PRESS

About Wharton School Press

Wharton School Press, the book publishing arm of the Wharton School of the University of Pennsylvania, was established to inspire bold, insightful thinking within the global business community.

Wharton School Press publishes a select list of award-winning, best-selling, and thought-leading books that offer trusted business knowledge to help leaders at all levels meet the challenges of today and the opportunities of tomorrow. Led by a spirit of innovation and experimentation, Wharton School Press leverages ground-breaking digital technologies and has pioneered a fast-reading business book format that fits readers' busy lives, allowing them to swiftly emerge with the tools and information needed to make an impact. Wharton School Press books offer guidance and inspiration on a variety of topics, including leadership, management, strategy, innovation, entrepreneurship, finance, marketing, social impact, public policy, and more.

Wharton School Press also operates an online bookstore featuring a curated selection of influential books by Wharton School faculty and Press authors published by a wide range of leading publishers.

To find books that will inspire and empower you to increase your impact and expand your personal and professional horizons, visit *wsp.wharton.upenn.edu.*

Wharton
UNIVERSITY of PENNSYLVANIA

About the Wharton School

Founded in 1881 as the world's first collegiate business school, the Wharton School of the University of Pennsylvania is shaping the future of business by incubating ideas, driving insights, and creating leaders who change the world. With a faculty of more than 235 renowned professors, Wharton has 5,000 undergraduate, MBA, executive MBA, and doctoral students. Each year 13,000 professionals from around the world advance their careers through Wharton Executive Education's individual, company-customized, and online programs. More than 100,000 Wharton alumni form a powerful global network of leaders who transform business every day. For more information, visit *www.wharton.upenn.edu.*